W9-AYR-443

HOW TO
FIX A
FACTORY

A practical approach to clarify and resolve
underlying challenges in your factory

Rob Tracy

A LEADER IN MANUFACTURING OPERATIONS FOR 30 YEARS

Copyright © 2019 by Rob Tracy.

All rights reserved. This book or any portion thereof may not be reproduced or used in any manner whatsoever without the express written permission of the publisher except for the use of brief quotations in a book review.

Publishing Services provided by Paper Raven Books

Printed in the United States of America

First Printing, 2019

Hardcover ISBN: 978-1-7333065-0-8
Paperback ISBN: 978-1-7333065-1-5

This book is dedicated to my wonderful wife, Liz, and our four children: Matt, Christine, Lauren, and Eric. Thank you for your support, love, patience, and tolerance. I couldn't have done this without you.

I almost forgot Lily, my six-year-old yellow lab. If it weren't for your help and incessant need for attention, this would have been done six months earlier.

TABLE OF CONTENTS

INTRODUCTION

Every factory will eventually run into trouble. Operations can be running smoothly, and then something happens. Before you know it, things aren't going so well. It can happen quickly, or it can creep up on you slowly. If you're the leader of a manufacturing operation, you know what this feels like. It feels broken. Systems and processes that used to get the job done are struggling. You're getting more customer complaints and frustrations are on the rise. It's not a lack of effort or desire, but something is wrong with the old formula for running the plant and it doesn't seem to improve no matter what you try. Out of desperation, you fall into one of two modes: You give in and resolve yourself to the misery of the daily battle or you throw a bunch of stuff at the wall and hope that something sticks.

I know. I've been there, and I'll share some of my experiences throughout the book.

The good news is that there is hope. In the coming pages, I'll share a path that will guide you out of the mess to stable footing and peace of mind. There will be plenty of heavy lifting, and there will be days when emotions run high. It will be worth it.

When you emerge, you'll have a healthier factory and you'll be a better leader. As the African proverb states: smooth seas do not make skillful sailors.

You may notice that this book contains very few references to Lean, which is the long-standing gold standard for excellence in manufacturing. I think Lean is great, but there is a difference between fixing the factory and striving towards excellence. Fixing the factory is focused on establishing a healthy, balanced, stable platform. There have been volumes written about how to become world-class, particularly using Lean techniques and philosophies, but that body of knowledge presumes a stable platform on which to build. Struggling manufacturers often look to leading excellence concepts, like Lean, to fix their factories, only to find their situation getting even worse. Manufacturers must get the fundamentals right before they attempt a more aggressive improvement method in search of excellence. It is the equivalent of working on core strength and flexibility before engaging an intense training program.

I've written this book with senior leaders in mind because they can influence change. I hope that others, like plant managers, production managers, and supervisors, also get value. However, to address the underlying issues that may be inhibiting performance the big dogs will need to step in.

The title of the book is *How to Fix a Factory*, and I say that somewhat tongue-in-cheek. All factories need fixing to some degree, but it's a spectrum. There are factories that get into really tough situations where nothing seems to be going right, and there are others that just need a little fine-tuning.

It is the difference between a car with a cracked windshield and a car with no brakes hurtling down a mountain pass road. The cracked windshield is an annoyance and it should be fixed, but the car is still drivable. The car with no brakes is in imminent danger and it's getting worse by the minute.

Some examples of situations that constitute "fixing" include:

- On-time delivery that isn't meeting customer expectations

- A workforce that is disengaged and going through the motions

- A cost position that isn't enabling sales and profitability

- Difficulty capturing and sustaining the gains of continuous improvement activities

- High inventories while experiencing stock-outs

- Reactive scheduling—running the plant from "hot lists"

- Capital investments in equipment that don't seem to be paying off

- Erratic financial performance

If the degree of "fixing" required in your facility is minor, you may be able to skip over some sections of the book. I've written the book to address plants that have spun out of control and the team members are feeling the pressure of the chaos and hopelessness of no end in sight.

Why Me

I made a career out of fixing factories. I didn't seek out this path. It seemed to find me. My first significant factory fix was at a window company in Ontario, Canada. It had fallen on hard times, and my employer, Andersen Windows, acquired it. At 32 years old, I was asked to turn it around and I did. It wasn't pretty, and if I could do it over there are many things that I'd do differently. But that's where I got bit by two bugs.

The first bug was a passion for small-and mid-size manufacturers. I enjoyed leading a business as opposed to running a department in a larger company. In a smaller company, you can move fast and you own your decisions. There's no place to run and no place to hide. I loved it.

The second bug was the rush and exhilaration that comes from fixing struggling factories. The journey is always hard, but the emotional rewards are great. I live for the feeling I get when I watch a frustrated, demoralized workforce get their mojo back. Thus far, I've had a direct impact on over a dozen operations. In most of those factories, I was a senior leader in the company with titles like VP of Operations, COO, or CEO. I've also helped numerous plants in a consulting capacity. My track record is heavily skewed towards successful fixes, but it isn't flawless. I've had a couple of factories that I haven't been able to turn and, as is often the case, I learned more from these than from the successes.

Nobody taught me how to do the factory fixes. There's no course on it. The lessons in this book were learned through real-life experience and the wisdom of some great mentors.

Your time is valuable, and I appreciate you sharing some of it with me. Let's get to work.

The Roadmap: An Overview

Creating a great manufacturing facility isn't complicated, but it's hard. What is required is a focus on operational health. It takes commitment to build a factory and a company that is truly solid, and it demands leadership, follow-through, perseverance, and investment. There is no easy path, but if you wanted the easy path you wouldn't be in manufacturing. I hope to demystify an approach to building a robust, rock-solid plant. It may not win awards for best in show, but it will deliver consistent results, and if you want to go further with Lean and other advanced techniques, you'll be prepared to do that.

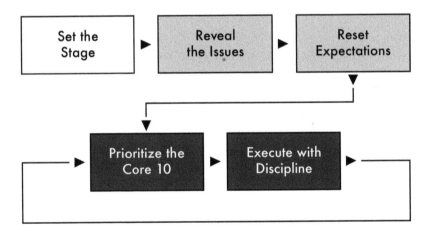

In this book, I'll describe the five elements of my approach to fixing a factory. The elements are:

Set the Stage	During recovery from distress, leadership must adopt a style that is confident *and* compassionate, resolute *and* vulnerable, and challenging without being overbearing.
Reveal the Issues	The next step is to understand the factors that are leading to challenges in the factory. These issues may be self-evident, but they might also require a peeling of the proverbial onion. This phase brings the issues, most of which are already known to the company, to the surface so that they can be confronted.
Reset Expectations	The journey toward improvement starts with stability. A stable environment is one that does not feel chaotic. In this phase, we reset expectations throughout the company and with customers to reflect the reality of the situation.
Prioritize the Core 10	A factory is comprised of systems and processes that must be working at a threshold level of performance. In this phase, we'll assess 10 core processes to determine which ones are having the biggest impact on the performance of the factory. This illuminates where we need to focus.
Execute with Discipline	Executing with discipline puts the great ideas identified in the prior steps to work. This is a hands-on manifestation of the Plan-Do-Check-Adjust cycle.

The remaining sections of this book will explore each of these five elements in greater detail.

SETTING THE STAGE

Fixing a factory requires a change in direction and momentum, and that change will only happen if the leadership team and the workforce are ready to embrace change and unite towards a common goal. Leading an organization from distress to health will challenge even the best leaders. When factories are struggling, people feel like they're playing a losing game. That needs to change.

In Greek mythology, Sisyphus is an evil king, and Zeus punishes him by making him push a boulder up a mountain every day. However, just as it gets to the top it rolls back to the bottom, and Sisyphus must repeat the agonizing push again the next day, and the next day, forever. This punishment, the daily grind of futile labor, was considered hideous. People working in a struggling factory can feel the same demoralizing effect. They come into work every day to a system that isn't working, and they grind it out. When they go home, they are tired, frustrated, and burdened with the feeling that tomorrow will be no better.

The Sisyphus dilemma must be broken. If it isn't, the factory challenges will only worsen. People will fall into a blaming mode and stop cooperating. They will be in a fearful mindset instead of a problem-solving mindset. Some will even choose to quit, taking valuable knowledge and insight with them. It is leadership's job to break the Sisyphus trap. The workforce will be thirsty for substantive hope that things are going to improve, and when they see it, they'll rally behind it. The key is that it must be substantive. Rah-rah speeches, posters, and platitudes will not suffice. It's going to take visible, tangible action.

Setting the Stage: Rubber Raft Leadership

When a factory needs fixing, the senior leadership team plays the crucial role of steering the ship and setting the tone for the organization. Leading an organization out of the chaos of being distressed towards being a healthy, vibrant, stable factory is a very different challenge than managing a high-performance organization.

Consider the difference between piloting a racing shell on the Charles River in Boston and piloting a rubber raft on the rapids of the Colorado River.

The racing shell is a long, narrow boat built for speed. There are rowers propelling the boat with oars, and the coxswain sitting at the rear of the boat steers it and barks out the rowing rhythm. I always enjoy watching these races in the summer Olympics. Finely tuned and highly trained athletes pull the oars in harmony, propelling a graceful boat across mirror-calm waters at amazing speeds. The racing shell is often held up as a model of high-performance teamwork. The coxswain is facing the rowers, calling stroke, stroke, stroke, and the rowers respond. This system works well on calm waters when you want to travel fast in a straight line.

However, if you put that racing shell on the whitewater rapids of the Colorado River, it will be smashed to bits in minutes. On the Colorado River, the rubber raft is the boat of choice. It is an ugly, slow beast that is difficult to maneuver, but it is flexible. It can take a lot of abuse, and in the hands of a skilled guide it can navigate raging waters and get the crew to the safety of calm waters farther down the river. The guide of a rubber raft barely has control of the boat. His single paddle has little impact, so he needs to motivate his crew, many of whom are complete novices, to paddle aggressively on one side or the other to try to avoid the rocks. And when someone goes overboard, the guide grabs them and hauls them back into the boat. After a quick check to make sure they're okay, he puts a paddle back in their hands because there's work to be done.

Leading a factory that is struggling is rubber raft leadership. The precision of a racing shell can come later. Leaders who have been accustomed to the role of the coxswain are going to need to adjust their style to become a rubber raft guide. There are three factors that embody rubber raft leadership:

1. Inspiration for the mission

2. Senior leader engagement

3. Leadership style

Inspiration for the mission:

If we want to break out of the Sisyphus punishment, the workforce must believe that their efforts are going to get the company to a better place in the future. People will do amazing things when they believe that they are part of building something special.

The inspiring message is not a single event, a single speech, or a single memo. It should be a series of messages that are woven into multiple communication methods. There should be a steady drip of communication through a variety of communication channels, including newsletters, daily tier meetings, staff meetings, special messages from the CEO, etc.

Communicating an inspiring message reminds me of the Stockdale Paradox. In *Good to Great*, Jim Collins wrote about his interview with Admiral James Stockdale, the senior ranking officer in the Hanoi prisoner-of-war camp in North Vietnam.

Admiral Stockdale spent seven years in the camp and he was tortured numerous times. Life in the prison was horrific—beyond what most of us can comprehend. Collins asked how he survived, and Stockdale replied, "Despite all those circumstances, I never ever wavered in my absolute faith that not only would I prevail—get out of this—but I would also prevail by turning it into the defining event of my life that would make me a stronger and better person."

Collins questioned him further by asking who didn't make it out, and Admiral Stockdale said, "The optimists. Yes. They were the ones who always said, 'We're going to be out by Christmas.' Christmas would come, and it would go. And there would be another Christmas. And they died of a broken heart. This is what I learned from those years in the prison camp, where all those constraints just were oppressive. You must never, ever, ever confuse, on the one hand, the need for absolute, unwavering faith that you can prevail despite those constraints with, on the other hand, the need for the discipline to begin by confronting the brutal facts, whatever they are. We're not getting out of here by Christmas."

The inspiring message to the workforce must confront this paradox. It must communicate faith that you'll get through the challenges while simultaneously facing the harsh realities of the current situation. People will look you in the eyes to see if you're for real or not. If they trust you, they'll get on board and engage to make things better. If they don't, they'll punch the clock and go back to being Sisyphus.

There are clearly nuances to the messaging. If the positive messages are overblown, they will sound like rhetoric from disconnected executives. If they are too weak, people will remain uninspired or perhaps even fearful. It's a fine line to walk. There must be acknowledgment and honesty about the current situation, combined with a steadfast resolve that better times are ahead. I think the reception of the message is going to be dependent on the trust that has been built up over the previous years. If the trust level is strong, they'll embrace what you're saying. If the trust level is weak, there's not much you can say that will sway them, and when that is the case the only thing to do is roll up your sleeves and show them.

An inspiring message often contains the following ingredients:

- An admission of the difficult situation that the company is facing. The people will want to know that you get it and you don't have your head in the sand.

- An expression of confidence that the company will prevail. All companies go through difficult times, and this is our turn. We'll get through it.

- A description of the specific actions that are being taken to correct the situation.

- A "silver lining" message about how the challenges are forcing us to build muscle that will make us stronger. Processes that have been issues for years bit us in the ass, and now we're fixing them. There are painful lessons being learned that are going to make us much stronger going forward.

- A perspective confirming that customers, shareholders, and suppliers all understand that difficult times happen. Our partners are still with us and they will be there as we emerge from this, *if* we band together and show the true spirit of our company and our people.

- News about victories that indicate that you're making progress.

- A reminder of the responsibility that we bear to each other, our families, and the community.

- A subtle warning that difficult times reveal character. It's time to show the world our real character. Our values still hold true. Let's remember to…(insert your three or four core values here).

- A heartfelt thank you.

Returning to the rubber raft analogy, this is the equivalent of the guide sitting everyone down prior to the next day's ride. He tells them that they're going to experience some of the most intense rapids on the river, and it's entirely possible that someone will go overboard. They have nothing to worry about. He's been through it many times before, and they'll be okay. They may get a little banged up, and they'll definitely be tired, but they'll be okay. When it's over, they'll look back on it as one of the most exhilarating events of their lives, and they may have a few scars to show for it, too.

Senior leader engagement:

Fixing factories is not a spectator sport. Every member of the senior leadership team needs to be a guide on the rubber raft. They aren't passengers in a boat or, worse yet, on the shore just observing.

One of my favorite quotes is from a speech that Teddy Roosevelt delivered in Paris, France in 1910.

> *It is not the critic who counts; not the man who points out how the strong man stumbles, or where the doer of deeds could have done them better. The credit belongs to the man who is actually in the arena, whose face is marred by dust and sweat and blood; who strives valiantly; who errs, who comes short again and again, because there is no effort without error and shortcoming; but who does actually strive to do the deeds; who knows great enthusiasms, the great devotions; who spends himself in a worthy cause; who at the best knows in the end the triumph of high achievement, and who at the worst, if he fails, at least fails while daring greatly, so that his place shall never be with those cold and timid souls who neither know victory nor defeat.*

If the company already has an aligned leadership team that has forged high levels of trust, engagement and mutual support will come naturally.

By contrast, companies in which the leadership team has relatively low team health, senior leaders often assume a blaming posture. If the leadership team is political, siloed, and distrustful, there is a taller mountain to climb. The sales team will blame the factory for poor customer service, and they'll warn of not being able to hit their numbers due to operations. The finance people may blame operations for poor financial performance, and HR may blame the factory for low morale and high turnover. Of course, the operations team is also tossing grenades. They'll accuse sales of not providing a good forecast and claim that HR isn't hiring the right people. They'll say that finance imposes the wrong metrics, and engineering is designing unmanufacturable parts. In short, everyone is blaming everyone in an effort to position themselves for survival through the maelstrom. In these environments, energy is being expended to fight the enemy within the organization. This is both unfortunate and unwise. In these situations, I recommend that the top dog responsible for the struggling factory (CEO, GM, division president) enlist the help of an expert in leadership team health to attempt to address this situation. A dysfunctional leadership team will exacerbate the issues, whereas a high-performing leadership team will accelerate the recovery.

As the leadership team works through the process of fixing a factory, which we'll cover in subsequent chapters, it's normal for every function in the organization to play a role in the recovery. Here are some examples of responsibilities that each department may need to carry:

CEO	Active communication and leadership. Running interference with key stakeholders such as owners, banks, key customers, and key suppliers.
Sales	Proactive, positive communication with customers.
Engineering	Addressing the design and manufacturing process issues that are contributing to the performance of the factory.
Purchasing	Proactively communicating with suppliers to keep them aligned and loyal. Addressing performance issues that are contributing to the challenges.
HR	Leading employee communication and assisting line leadership with change management.
Finance	Developing key metrics that are aligned with the recovery. Developing financial forecasts that reflect the reality of the situation.
IT	Improving responsiveness to IT reliability issues. Addressing systems and processes that are contributing to the issues.
Manufacturing	Implementing the shop floor improvements to correct the situation. Ensuring daily execution of objectives and leading the workforce.

The senior leadership team can follow one of two paths. They can unite towards leading the company through the rapids or they can fragment and become divisive, blaming, and territorial.

Leadership teams that unite have great odds of working through their challenges, and leadership teams that fragment will prolong their pain.

Leadership style:

Early in my career, I was discussing leadership styles with a mentor. I asked him, "What is the best leadership style?" He answered, "The best leadership style is the style that the organization needs right now." This was great advice, and it's particularly relevant if you need to lead an organization through turbulent waters.

There have been countless books written on leadership styles, so I won't rehash them. What I would like to do is paint a picture of the style that I've seen work well, and the whitewater guide analogy is illustrative.

Consider the guides that you may have worked with in the past. It doesn't have to be whitewater rafting, but it needs to be a guide who has taken you on an adventure that has an element of danger if not done well. It could be a fishing guide, hunting guide, or hiking guide. I've used a few myself, and here are the things that I liked about the best guides and their corollaries to leadership:

Category	Guides	Business Leaders
Safety	The guide emphasizes the key elements of safety. He understands the concerns of the people he's guiding, and he is direct and candid about what people need to do to stay safe. If people behave unsafely, he corrects it immediately.	The senior leadership team needs to ensure that physical safety remains a top priority, but it also needs to create an environment of emotional safety. Creating an atmosphere that is free of blame and focused on the future can put people at ease.
Competence	The guide demonstrates that he has the experience, knowledge, and capability to lead them on the journey down the river.	If you are competent and capable, then your people will already know it. However, I don't want to pull punches here. If you are unsure about how to navigate these rapids, get help. Your team will applaud you for being self-aware enough to know where you're strong and where you're not.

Category	Guides	Business Leaders
Social	The guide keeps things fun. When times get hard, like when everyone is soaking wet and cold, the guide knows how to lighten the mood, even if that involves a bit of eccentricity.	The leadership team needs to introduce fun. Smiles and laughter go a long way towards rebuilding energy and engagement. It's easy for leaders to get into a funk given the pressures they face but introducing some regular fun breaks is great for everyone's mental health.
Focus	While the guide has a lighthearted demeanor, he doesn't lose sight of the mission. He needs to go get everyone to the pickup point safe and sound by a designated time. The guide isn't heavy-handed about this, but he ensures that the crew understands what must happen.	The management team needs to provide clarity about the primary objective so that everyone knows what they are striving towards. They must state a goal that says that the company must go from result A to result B, by mm/dd/yy. This objective must provide the anchor for all other activities.

Category	Guides	Business Leaders
Engaging	A great guide assesses his guests and meets them where they're at without judgment. If they need a lot of support, he provides it, and if they are self-sufficient, he lets them do their thing. In all cases, he strives to make sure that the success of the outing is because of them, not him.	The leadership team also meets people where they are to help them on the journey. Punitive actions and discipline are reserved for only egregious situations. The leadership team is going out of its way to make sure that people are on the journey with them.

Rubber raft leadership: Wrap-up

The senior leadership team plays an instrumental role in creating an environment that will respond and rise to the challenges of a factory that needs fixing. It requires the engagement, not just the support, of each member of the leadership team. The senior leadership team establishes the tone and tenor that will energize people for a journey that is bound to meet with rocks in the water, and they help the organization remain tough and resilient—like a rubber raft.

Setting the Stage: Baseline of Respect

Companies that demonstrate a deep respect for people have a tremendous advantage when it comes time to fix the factory.

When the workforce senses they are respected, they will trust that the changes being implemented are for the greater good and they'll engage to be part of the solution. In the paragraphs that follow, you will find me using respect and engagement interchangeably because I think the two are intrinsically linked. There can be no engagement without respect, and deep respect almost always engenders engagement.

Looking inside: How do you really feel?

Demonstrating respect for people is a very personal interaction. While companies may have policies that are generally respectful, deep respect is personal. It comes down to people judging whether they respect the other party and whether they believe the other party respects them.

We've all heard the clichés: "We empower our people" and "People are our greatest asset." Often these are nothing more than corporate wallpaper. They are slogans that sound good but have not been put into action. If every company that espoused how much they value their employees walked the talk, we wouldn't have a 12 percent engagement rate with manufacturing employees.[1]

The employee survey can be another example of companies giving surface treatment to demonstrating respect. There is often a flurry of activity around survey time, as the surveys are distributed, completed, analyzed, and then acted on. The problem is that the "acted on" phase is often shallow, mechanical, and short-lived. As soon as the next crisis comes along, leadership resorts to prior behaviors, and attention shifts from heavy lifting that must be done to show respect and earn engagement.

[1] 2017 Gallup State of the Global Workforce Report

The transient and superficial attempts at demonstrating respect reflect the underlying beliefs of leadership. Every company that I've seen with a high level of employee engagement has a leader, and leadership team, that deeply believes in the strength and value of their employees. It's more than a strategic imperative, or something that they feel like they need to do to address hiring and retention issues; it's deep within them. It's in their hearts, not just their minds.

I was speaking with the CEO of a very successful, family-owned manufacturing company that had a unique perk for their employees. They owned a vacation resort on a lake in northern Wisconsin and they would let the employees use it. There were several small cabins and access to pontoon boats and other recreational activities. All of this was provided at no cost to the employees. I commented to the owner, "It is nice that you have a financial position strong enough to be able to provide this great benefit for your employees," and he quickly corrected me by saying, "Rob, you have it backward. We have great results *because* we do these things for our employees."

This raises a question for anyone leading people. How do you *really* feel about your employees? I'm not asking how you think about your employees or where employees fit in your strategic plan. I'm asking how you feel. This can be hard to confront because I think we know how we're supposed to feel, but it may not be reflected in our deep-down views—the views that we probably wouldn't say out loud.

One of the things that I do when I first engage with the client is listen to the words that are used in reference to their employees. Examine the contrast in these statements—all spoken from the point of view of manager or leader:

A Low-Respect Leader	A High-Respect Leader
Laborer	Teammate
They are resistant to change.	We haven't resolved the employees' underlying concerns.
They've had it really good for a long time, and now they feel entitled.	I can understand why they are concerned. We've been successful for a long time, and they want to see that continue.
We have a bunch of employees who have been here a long time, and they don't want to change.	We are blessed with an experienced workforce. We need to figure out how to tap into their knowledge.
The supervisors are really weak.	We haven't invested in our supervisors. They have a really tough job.
They're just a temp.	Every person who works here is part of our team.
People resist change.	People don't resist change; they resist being changed. We need to include them in the process.
What kind of incentive should we offer? They'll only respond to dollars.	Money incentives are superficial and short-lived. What can we do to win their hearts and minds?
People quit because they can get another job for $0.25/hour more down the road.	If people are quitting for $0.25, we're doing something wrong as leaders.
This new generation just doesn't want to work.	Every generation thinks the next generation has gone to hell, and it's not right to paint everyone with the same brush. We need to adapt and figure out how to engage them.

The comments in the left-hand column are common, and it's rare to find companies framing statements like those in the right-hand column. The big distinction between a low-respect leader and a high-respect leader is that the low-respect leader implicitly blames the people while the other is looking inwardly at the leadership. This difference illuminates the bias in the minds of the leaders.

If you have created a culture of respect over the years, then you have a good head start on the ability to implement change rapidly. However, if you and your company have a history of showing a lack of respect for workers, then you have a bigger task at hand. It is unlikely that you'll be able to completely turn the tables and change the level of mutual respect, but you can make progress. There is an old Chinese proverb that says, "When is the best time to plant a tree? Thirty years ago. When is the second-best time to plant a tree? Today."

If you've done some soul searching and have discovered that you have some low-respect tendencies you want to shift, there are concrete steps you can take. Our biases towards our workforce are not hardwired in our DNA. They are malleable with practice. Here are a few recommendations for starting to change your mindset:

- Practice catching yourself and your leadership team using low-respect language. The discipline of intentionally listening for the verbal cues will be enlightening, as it's a window into your thought process. The philosopher Lao Tzu said,

Watch your thoughts, they become your words; watch your words, they become your actions; watch your actions, they become your habits; watch your habits, they become your character; watch your character, it becomes your destiny.

- Enlist the help of others. While I don't recommend standing up in front of the whole workforce and proclaiming a new attitude of respect, I do think it makes sense to confide in a few people. Tell them that you're trying to change and ask for their input and support. Let them know that you want feedback, both positive and negative, about how you're doing. Besides getting honest feedback, you'll receive the secondary benefit of the grapevine. If you enlist the help of a few key influencers, the word will get out that you're trying. Twitter has nothing on the speed of the rumor mill in factories.

- Hire a coach to work with the leadership team. A good coach, preferably with an organizational development or psychology background, could help you explore, understand, and break through your biases. This person would also likely be able to help with other aspects of the change that you're seeking to bring about.

Looking inside and questioning your own thoughts, biases, and perspectives is difficult, maybe even gut-wrenching. You may view yourself as a people-person who trusts and values your people, but upon reflection you find out that maybe it's not quite as true as you thought. That's okay. In fact, just having that open and honest view of yourself is half the battle. We may not be able to change our height or even some parts of our personality, but we *can* change our thoughts.

I went through this early in my career. I was leading a team of people and we weren't getting along. It started to turn ugly. I was complaining about "them" and my team was complaining about me. I was fortunate that my boss decided to invest heavily in me and hired a coach. I went through a process of discovery that has impacted me to this day. I remember one day when he was shadowing me in a staff meeting. I thought it was a pretty good meeting. We got a lot done, and there was joking and laughing. I expected to get accolades from the coach. After the meeting, he pulled me aside, and he gently said, "I think you need to knock off the locker room humor. I'm not talking about sexual innuendos or anything. There was none of that, but the teasing and jabbing and sparring that goes on with you and some of the guys is alienating about half your team. The women, in particular, didn't care for it. Did you notice how they went quiet every time you guys started sparring? You will build a healthier team if you stop doing it."

That conversation, and many others with my coach, shaped who I am today. I'm far from perfect—just ask anyone who has worked for me. I still like to tease, and I occasionally need to be reminded about it, but I try (I grew up in a family that teased each other incessantly). It was a difficult and emotional process to go through. I had to lower my guard, be vulnerable, and deeply listen to what I was being told. And despite the difficulty, or perhaps because of it, having a coach was one of the best growth experiences of my life.

Your workforce will only become highly engaged if you truly want them engaged. It starts with demonstrating deep respect.

Actions to demonstrate respect

Once you are past the soul searching, there are concrete actions you can take to demonstrate your respect for the workforce. Some of these things may sound like they should take a back seat when the factory is struggling. I encourage you to think differently. Doing some of these things sends a strong message to your people. It says that even in times of turmoil, we're going to continue to do things that demonstrate our respect for you because it means that much to us.

- Live your values

  Hopefully you have defined your values and you've shared them with the workforce. Make sure that you're living them. Hire, promote, and fire based on them. If a person doesn't fit your values, get them on a path to change or leave the company. Firing toxic people is one of the best ways to earn the trust of your workforce.

- Clean factory

  People like working in a clean factory. Walk through the plant with a couple of employees and listen to what bothers them. It may be all of the dust, or restrooms that are gross on the second shift, or chewing tobacco containers, or some mold and mildew in the refrigerators in the breakroom. Note that this is different from a full-blown 5S program, like one might implement as part of a Lean implementation. 5S is much more than making a factory clean and safe, and while 5S is awesome, we don't need to go that far in order to demonstrate respect. This is focused on making the factory a decent place to come to every day.

- Upgrade the facility

A close corollary to creating a clean factory is to do some modest building upgrades.

I have been in factories that have leaky roofs dripping water where workers are working, and I've seen restrooms that make you wonder if washing your hands will make you cleaner or dirtier. There are break rooms that cram people into dilapidated areas with refrigerators that don't work. I was even in a building where the overhead office lights were 50 percent broken and employees were working in the dark.

Those are examples of the non-production areas, but these issues extend into the production areas as well. Asking people to fight with a piece of equipment that is old, worn, and can no longer do the job is inherently disrespectful. And allowing known safety hazards to exist sends an implied message about how you value your workforce, whether you intend to send that message or not.

Imagine that you are a worker in one of these environments. Someone from high in the organization comes to you and gives a great presentation about how employees are the greatest asset and say they want to empower you and engage with you to achieve a grand strategic plan. How would you feel? I have to believe that skepticism would be one of the mildest reactions, and flat-out anger would be a common one. I can't tell you how many times I've heard things like, "Oh...we can afford to spend a bunch of money on the new marketing hot shot, or the ad campaign, but you can't fix my bathroom?"

This issue gets magnified when there is a wide disparity between the accommodations of the offices and the factory. When shop floor people see the office getting investment in new furniture and fixtures while they're taking a break on chairs that have duct-tape on them, it is hard for them to believe that you really care about them and that you view them as humans who you value. The message being sent is, "You're a pawn and just a laborer."

The one situation in which you can get away with this is if your company has been in financial distress. In that case, you can ask for forgiveness and communicate that you *want* them to have better working conditions and you're committed to it, but you just don't have the money. And you need their help and engagement in order to get in a better position to be able to pay for the improvements.

You don't need to make all the changes at once. The employees will respond when they see that you're taking steps to improve their environment. When you show them the roadmap of the improvements that you intend to make, they will cut you a lot of slack.

The facility and the environment that you create for employees is a physical manifestation of how you feel about them. If you want them engaged with you, create an environment that tells them that.

- Provide transparent communication

  Openly sharing information signals to the workforce that you trust them to use the information as thinking, mindful adults. For example, family-owned companies can be concerned about sharing profitability numbers, thinking that the employees will view them as greedy, rich people. However, some of the strongest privately held companies that I've seen openly share their profitability. They teach their employees about how profits get reinvested in the business and how profitability helps to keep them strong and sustainable.

- Implement listening sessions

  One of the greatest signs of respect for people is to listen to them. One client conducted monthly "What's on your mind" lunches. They would gather employees who were celebrating an anniversary to have lunch, and they'd ask the open-ended question, "What's on your mind?" These always started out a little slow, but then they would evolve into very healthy discussions. During these lunches, the leadership team went in with the mindset of "I'm here to learn and listen...not to defend, convince, or sell."

- Know each person's name

  Knowing a person's name shows them that you respect them and, likewise, not knowing their name is taken as a strong sign of disrespect. You can picture an employee going home after a long day, sitting down at the dinner table saying, "You know, I don't think they know my name. I'm just a number to them."

- Involve them in problem-solving

  People can tell whether you view them as part of the problem or part of the solution. When you include them as part of the problem-solving process, they will know that you value them for more than their labor. This can be incorporated into daily management practices, like the shiftly stand-up meeting.

Having an environment of respect for employees enables rapid change and, when factories need to be fixed, faster change means a faster return to health. However, respect can't be faked. It needs to be present in the hearts and minds of leadership, and it must be demonstrated through both actions and words.

Park Industries

I've had the honor of serving on the board at Park Industries. Park has been in business since 1953, and they are now in their third generation of ownership. They're a mid-size manufacturer with about 300 employees in the central Minnesota city of St. Cloud.

The St. Cloud area is known for its granite quarries, and companies have sprung up in the area to support the granite industry. Park is one of them. They started by making simple hydraulic splitters, but as stone grew in popularity for home construction, new opportunities emerged. Rather than just support the quarries, they decided to design and build the equipment used to cut the stone. This equipment is purchased by the countertop shops in local communities across the United States.

The machines they make are engineered precisely, built beautifully, and supported passionately. Even with all of these great achievements, what impresses me the most about Park is their relationship with their people.

Tom Schlough, the founder's son, former CEO and current board chairman, instilled a deep caring for people that lives on in the organization. We were discussing culture at a board meeting, and Tom said, "Everybody out on that floor is somebody's son or daughter. When they are at the dinner table with their parents and they're asked, 'How's it going at work?' I want them to be able to tell them what a great place this is. That's what I'd want my kids to be able to say about their employer."

The housing market crash of 2008 was both a trial and a testament to their relationship with the workforce. When housing starts plummeted from 2.2 million per year to 475,000 per year, orders for stone-cutting equipment nearly evaporated. Nobody needed more equipment, and Park was thrust into a fight for survival. Costs had to come down or bankruptcy would be inevitable. They had no choice but to lay off a large chunk of their workforce. In fact, they had to cut nearly two-thirds of their employees. It was gut-wrenching, but they could see no way to avoid it.

The remaining employees all shared in the pain. There were pay cuts for all salaried people, and the production workforce went on a reduced schedule. When this was happening, nobody knew how bad it was going to get or how long it was going to last. It was fighting to live another day. When leaders would run into laid-off workers at the grocery store, the prevailing sentiment was, "It's really tough, but we don't blame you. You just did what you had to do."

One aspect of how they handled the crisis gives great insight into the trust that they place in their people. They had a long-held practice of sharing financial information with their employees. Typically, they did this in all-employee meetings where the company leaders would present the information. Let's pause right there—a privately held company shared confidential financial information with the employees. They didn't need to do that, and there are always concerns about employees misinterpreting the information and viewing the owners as greedy. Instead of fearing that perception, they believed that their people would understand the financials if they were explained well, and they trusted the employees to keep it confidential.

During the housing meltdown, as they were laying off people and taking pay cuts, they decided that it wasn't appropriate to share information quarterly. They decided to share it *monthly*. The company leaders felt that the best way to win the hearts, minds, and loyalty of the remaining employees was to be 100 percent open and candid with them. This approach was instinctive to Park's leadership, but it flies in the face of conventional management practices.

Fast forward five years and the housing market had rebounded to about one million starts. Park survived and it was growing again. They called back their workers and all but five people returned. They wanted to be at Park!

When I first started working with Park, I wondered what the secret sauce was. It isn't the location. They're located in an industrial park with dozens of other businesses that are not reputed to have the same relationship with their workers. They pay competitive wages, but they are definitely not buying loyalty and engagement. The high value that they place on their employees is simply woven into their daily thinking and actions.

They have taken the time to document their beliefs about people and culture in "The Park Way." The Park Way is a very different document than the Toyota Way. The Park Way is a short document that describes their mission, values, and behaviors that they hold sacrosanct. It is reviewed with every employee annually. It is integrated into the processes for hiring and performance feedback. It is a management document that is reviewed annually with the board of directors. It is a serious document that describes the kind of culture they want.

The leadership team also takes many concrete actions to live the Park Way. Here are a few examples:

- Senior leadership is expected to know everybody's name in the company. In order to make that a reality, they create flashcards with everyone's name and picture, and they spend evenings at home reviewing the flashcards so that they can address every person on the floor by their name.

- The two top leaders (they have a unique co-president structure) write roughly 2,000 notes to their employees and families. Cards are sent on the associate's birthday, the spouse's birthday, and their work anniversary. The personal notes are sent to the associates' homes.

- They have a profit-sharing program that is tied to the health of the organization so that associates share in the success of the company.

- The cafeteria is self-vending and based on the honor system.

- All members of management are expected to participate in community activities, both on company time and personal time. These activities are reviewed with the board annually.

- The annual review of the top executives includes feedback from employees about the degree to which they are living the Park Way.

The list goes on and on, but copying these tactics will not be successful unless the top leadership has a deep belief in the power of building an incredible bond with employees.

For the skeptics among you that are rolling your eyes thinking that this is a country club company that doesn't manage performance or focus on profitability, I can also assure you that the company is rigorous in its strategic planning, governance, capital investment, and financial performance management. At Park, treating people with respect and dignity is not a trade-off with disciplined management; it is an integral part of disciplined management.

REVEAL THE ISSUES

Revealing the issues that are leading to the factory's struggles is the starting point of fixing a factory. It's the equivalent of giving the whole organization a shot of truth serum. We're going to question and explore until we have insight into what is really happening—not what we think should be happening or what the manual says. In most cases, people inside organizations know the issues, but for one reason or another they aren't rising to the surface so that they can be acted on.

A family-owned contract manufacturer was struggling with profitability, so they asked me to come in and take a look. I started with a discovery process, and after a few days I had a bad feeling. I pulled the CEO aside and said: "I don't know how to say this, but I think there is some fraud going on and I'm afraid that it may be your brother." His response surprised me. He shook his head and said, "I thought we had that fixed." Deep down, he knew what was going on. It was just too difficult to confront. There were family ties with spouses and kids involved. It was a very ugly situation.

I chose the word "reveal" for this purpose. It is rare for there to be a startling revelation. It is more common to confirm and shed light on suspicions and ideas that the team already harbors.

It reminds me of a dialogue with my oldest son, Matt. When he was seven or eight, we were driving through our suburban neighborhood around Christmas time, and he said, "Dad, tell me again how Santa gets to all of these houses. I don't understand." I decided to come clean and tell him about the myth of Santa and he shouted: "Dang, I knew it last year, but I was afraid to say anything."

The reticence to share openly happens inside of organizations, too. This is compounded by an unwillingness to listen openly. It's as if there's been a collective handshake to keep our heads in the sand. When we take part in the Reveal the Issues phase, we have to be intentional and deliberate about opening the communication channels.

Revealing the underlying issues can take some digging. A simple symptom, like poor on-time delivery, often has a number of causes. Maybe the plant is not making enough product, the scheduling systems are screwed up, or the customer service group accepted customer request dates without understanding plant capacity. The unfortunate reality is that we can't fix poor on-time delivery. We need to find the underlying factors negatively affecting on-time delivery and fix those.

I have been in factories that could be fixed by a small tweak in a process, and I've also been in factories where it seemed that every one of the core processes was broken. We won't know until we look.

In this section, I'll cover:

- Paradigm blind spots

- Denial

- Facing personal loss

- Using real numbers

- The process for gathering insights

- Sharing the findings—The Reveal

Reveal the Issues: Paradigms

The *Merriam-Webster Dictionary* defines a paradigm as an "example, pattern, especially: an outstandingly clear or typical example or archetype." We all have paradigms, and they are wonderful and necessary for making fast decisions. Paradigms often contain a commonly accepted body of knowledge. For example, prior to Copernicus, there was a paradigm that the sun and everything else revolved around the earth. We now know that the prior paradigm, the Ptolemaic model, was deeply flawed, but it was commonly accepted as the truth until Copernicus was able to shift the paradigm with his book *De revolutionibus orbium coelestium.*

Paradigms are powerful, but they can also create blind spots and obscure the truth. Studies have shown that we will filter out data that doesn't agree with our paradigms.

Let's use a well-known illusion to illustrate the power of paradigms. The image below shows a three-dimension representation of a checkerboard. At the corner of the checkerboard is a square that is casting a shadow over the checkerboard. Examine squares one and two closely. Would you believe me if I told you that they are the same color? They are. Even though I know the truth, I cannot get my brain to believe it. We have a paradigm about the effect of shadows on color, and we have a paradigm about the color patterns of a checkerboard. Without the use of a tool, I cannot get my brain to override those paradigms and let me truly see that the colors are the same. My guess is that a graphic artist, who has been trained to understand the nature of colors and the impact of shadows, might have no difficulty seeing that they are the same. They would be able to look past the illusion of three-dimensionality and shadows to see the real colors.

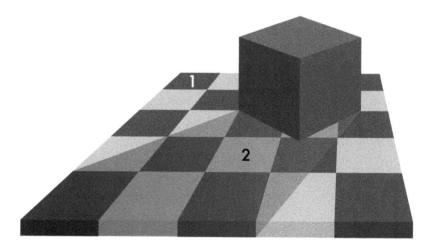

Here is an example of paradigms shaping the leader's perspective of the operation of the company.

Paradigm example: Equipment purchase

A manufacturer in Wisconsin was struggling with low profit margins. The tour guide, an engineer, showed me a new piece of equipment with obvious pride. He showed me how they were able to dramatically reduce costs on the part because they could run the part faster. His paradigm for achieving cost reduction was based on mass production and standard cost accounting. In this paradigm, less time per piece results in less overhead, which lowers the cost in the accounting system. In his mind, this was indisputable. The machine was faster and the costs in the accounting system showed solid improvement.

My paradigm is different, and it led me to ask a couple of questions to understand the benefit of the new equipment:

- Was the increased speed needed in order to keep up with customer demand? No.

- Is the new equipment more reliable than the old equipment? No, in fact it is finicky.

- Did you redeploy the worker to other areas after customer needs were met? No.

From my perspective, it would appear that purchasing this piece of equipment had a negative financial impact. There is no increase in revenue and no decrease in real costs. In fact, real costs likely went up due to the costs of maintenance and engineering support. Plus, valuable capital and time were spent on a project that wasn't going to move the needle.

I felt strongly that my paradigm was the correct view of the situation, but the engineer and cost accountants also felt strongly that they had the proper view. This example illustrates how the exact same facts can lead to dramatically different conclusions depending on one's paradigm.

Addressing paradigm blind spots

Paradigms can be quite problematic because no matter how open-minded we want to be, it can be nearly impossible to see our own paradigms. They tend to be accepted as givens. They represent the conventional wisdom that has been largely accepted as fact.

The only way that I know how to address paradigm blindness is to intentionally seek out the input and perspective of others and to establish a mindset of curiosity. There needs to be a willingness to deeply understand the other person's view of the situation. Ideally, the people providing the alternative perspective have already earned your respect and trust. They are likely to offer input that doesn't align with your natural biases, and a relationship of trust and respect will help bridge the gap so that there is an atmosphere of learning and exploration.

As the leader of your organization, it will be your call as to whether you choose to adopt the paradigm and worldview of the other party. After all, just because they have a different paradigm does not make their paradigm more valid than yours. A review of the track record of implementing the new paradigm may give some indication as to whether it is something you want to adopt.

Perhaps the most important aspect of paradigms is to be cognizant of the fact that they exist and can create blind spots.

This understanding will help you to face contrarian points of view with an inquisitive mind rather than immediately dismissing them as wrong.

Reveal the Issues: Denial

Another major challenge to revealing the issues in a factory is an unwillingness to confront very difficult or challenging topics. There are times when there is the proverbial elephant in the room and confronting it may mean facing something daunting.

One original equipment manufacturer (OEM) had suffered through nearly a decade of market share erosion. It was part of the persona of the company to make premium products, and yet lower-cost alternatives were steadily taking market share. The company tried a number of things, including developing a slightly less expensive option and international expansion, but nothing was changing the momentum of the market. During that decade of market share erosion, they knew what they needed to do. They needed to transition from two-step distribution to single-step distribution. The answer was obvious, but facing it was difficult because the choice was loaded with risks and challenges, including the alienation of most of their sales force. It took a high-powered strategy consulting firm to hit the executive team between the eyes and get them to face the reality of the situation. They could face the difficult decision or fade away into obscurity.

We're seeing this happen time and again with the changes that are unfolding in the retail arena. National retail chains are dropping like flies because they were unwilling to confront the realities of the changing retail market. Companies like Blockbuster, Barnes & Noble, Sears, and Toys "R" Us were all invested heavily in brick-and-mortar infrastructure, and the leap to an e-commerce model was too much to consider. They fought the good fight and tried to figure out how to fit into the new retail world, but they eventually lost. They weren't prepared to face the harsh realities of the situation.

Manufacturers are not immune to game-changing dynamics, and they can be just as stubborn as the retailers I've just mentioned. The challenges and issues impacting your operation may only require a minor tweak, but you should be mentally prepared to confront more significant issues. For example, a precision machine shop serving the aerospace industry in the Southwest was struggling with profitability. The reality of their situation was that their equipment was beyond the end of its useful life. The business was at a crossroad about whether to invest or fold, and that was their hard-to-confront reality. As difficult as it was, it was better to look the issue in the eye than to suffer a steady, predictable decline.

Addressing denial

Confronting a difficult issue usually requires the engagement of a trusted advisor. That person may be a Vistage coach, attorney, CPA, friend, or business advisor. There are two keys attributes that must exist:

1. You must have deep trust in this person. You must feel that even if this person says things that are difficult to absorb, they are only sharing them with you in order to help you.

2. The advisor must have good business acumen and

understand your business. If you are being told that there are significant issues that may require you to "bet the farm" to fix things, the advice needs to come from a person who understands your business.

Reveal the Issues: Personal Loss

The third area that can make it hard to reveal the issues is the loss that you might personally experience. It would be natural to have concerns about how you might personally be impacted if the issues were revealed. There could be a loss of status in the organization or potentially even a loss of job security.

I can tell you from firsthand experience that this is an uncomfortable situation. A number of times in my career, I've had to admit to myself, "I blew it; that was the wrong call and we're paying for it." One of my most vivid examples was a decision to close a factory and consolidate all operations from three factories into two. In order to do this, we needed to cut our inventories in half to create space, which meant that we needed to cut lot sizes in half. I arrogantly said, "We can do that. We'll just have to focus on setup reduction." The setup reduction turned out to be much more difficult than I had expected—a fact that the operators had warned me about. Our costs skyrocketed and on-time delivery plummeted. It took a couple of years to undo that mess. While it would have been easy to blame others—workers, engineers, and Lean specialists—the uncomfortable truth is that my decision was wrong. I was lucky to have a board of directors that tolerated that misstep; they treated my mistake as expensive tuition, but it created many sleepless nights for me and I'm sure that it influenced my perspectives and actions.

We've all heard that we learn more from our mistakes than from our successes, but it is also true that we get fired more often for our mistakes than our successes. A poster extolling the virtue of mistakes does little to curb the anxieties about the damage that may have been done to your career, status, and livelihood.

It's hard to admit that you may have been part of the problem. The difficult reality is that your leadership and decisions have likely contributed to this situation. Owning up to that truth requires incredible personal courage, especially knowing that doing so may impact your career. Unfortunately, some corporate environments do not treat missteps as a learning experience. Personal insecurities and fears can create great barriers to deeply understanding the current situation.

Addressing personal loss

Everyone makes mistakes throughout their career. If you've done something that has led to the challenges that are facing the factory, it's best to own up to them. When I sit on boards of directors, I listen intently to whether the business leaders are learning from their missteps. If they are learning, I cut them a lot of slack. If they are making excuses and deflecting the blame to others, like customers, the workforce, or the weather, then my antenna goes up and I start thinking that maybe we don't have the right person.

There's no guarantee that it will work out for you, but ignoring the issue and refusing to face the facts will only exacerbate the situation. Do the right thing. Confront the difficult situation. Take your lumps and move on. The quicker you own it, the quicker you can recover and move forward.

Reveal the Issues: Real Numbers

I was called into a contract manufacturer's facility because lead times had grown substantially over the prior six months and customers were upset. In addition to the long lead times, the factory was consistently missing delivery date promises. As part of the discovery process to reveal the issues, I attended a few meetings to see what data they were using. I heard about late deliveries, efficiencies, and production variances. What I didn't hear was the very basic data around how many widgets were supposed to be made and how many were actually produced. If the plant was supposed to make 10 widgets and it only made 8, it's going to fall behind. If that is repeated day after day, the plant is digging a deepening hole. Unfortunately, I see far too many environments where fundamental measurements have been eschewed in favor of technically accurate but completely unhelpful data.

When I enter a facility for the first time, I try to establish a base of real-life numbers, and I work hard to avoid using dollars as the unit of measure. Executives speak the language of dollars, but it tends to lose its meaning at lower levels of the organization. The executive team may say, "We need to be able to produce $5 million more per year," but companies produce products and not dollars. It is better to translate that goal into something tangible, such as, "We currently produce 10,000 widgets per year, and that needs to increase to 12,000 per year, which is an additional 8 widgets per day." This type of problem statement tends to help people grasp the context and magnitude of the issue more than using dollars.

Employee turnover might be another example. Most companies express turnover as a percentage. A company might say that they had turnover of 10.2 percent, and on the surface that doesn't sound too bad. However, rephrasing the question to get to real numbers puts the matter in a different light. If I say something like, "We've added about 20 people to the headcount over the last three years. How many people have we had to hire, both temps and regulars, to net those 20 people?" In this day and age, it would not surprise me to hear that the number is 100 or more. So, this company needs to hire 5 people to net 1 staff addition. Seeing it that way sheds light on the talent management challenge much more so than a sterilized 10.2 percent turnover rate.

Shown below are examples of the data that I commonly try to accumulate, usually with a 12- to 24-month history:

- How many products were made?

- How many products are customers asking for?

- How many people do we employ? How many do we need?

- Which processes are experiencing downtime? How much?

- How many people have been injured?

- What is the overtime rate?

- How many people have quit in the last year?

- How many days or weeks of inventory do we have?

- How many hours are we spending fixing defects?

While it's ideal to translate the data into non-financial metrics, there are times that there is no choice but to express the data using dollars. If one of the issues is related to financial performance, such as low profitability, work hard to use real numbers and not rely solely on conventions in the accounting system. One area of concern is product costing. While a full description of the issues with normal standards-based accounting systems is beyond the scope of this book, suffice it to say that reliance on product costs can be very misleading. In standard costing systems, overhead costs, which are a significant portion of the cost of a company, are allocated to products based on factors like labor hours or machine hours. This is an arbitrary method of spreading around costs. It gives the perception of accuracy, but that perception is an illusion. I recommend adopting a direct-costing or value-add approach for the financial analysis.

Direct costing attempts to distill costs down to the real dollars that are spent. Allocations and non-cash items, like depreciation and inventory adjustments, are removed from the analysis.

I was working with a large manufacturer to try to understand why they were experiencing profitability erosion. As part of that analysis, we charted the overhead costs by month. These were all costs except for materials and production labor. Usually, this bucket of costs is very stable month over month. It doesn't tend to fluctuate with volume like production costs. In this factory, we saw wild swings month to month, which was having a significant impact on the margins reported out of the factory. The swings in gross margin were giving senior management heartburn because they felt that the factory was out of control. After digging into it further, we found that accounting drove most of these fluctuations. They were adjusting accruals for bonuses and profit sharing, and they'd remove a bunch of accruals one month, only to add them back the next month. I've seen other factories where inventory adjustments had the same impact. These types of accounting adjustments muddy the analytical water and they need to be removed. Once we pulled out these adjustments, we had a clear picture of the situation. We learned that the factory had done a great job of controlling overhead costs, and we needed to look elsewhere to find the source of the profitability erosion.

Go See for Yourself

While it's important to use data and to be analytically rigorous, we mustn't forget the power of visual observation. When I am proposing on work for a client, I always require a plant tour before we get too far into the process. In a one-hour tour, you can often gain tremendous insights that will point you in a direction for the analysis. When I tour a shop with a plant manager, I can usually assess things like:

- Is the workforce productive? In other words, is the pace of work plodding or energized?

- Is the factory leadership disciplined? If the factory isn't clean, or people aren't wearing their personal protective equipment, or charts aren't updated, it's an indicator of a factory that is struggling with daily discipline.

- Is there a lot of inventory with thick dust? It might be an indicator of supply chain issues.

- Do people smile and wave when you go by, or do they flip you the bird with their eyes?

- The simple question, "How do they know if they're having a good day?" will shed light on whether it is a culture of engagement where the workers take ownership for their results.

Data is important, but remember the power of seeing, hearing, and sensing firsthand.

Reveal the Issues: The Process

If we accept that each of us will view the current situation with built-in and natural biases, the challenge is to go through a process of exploration and discovery that has the highest likelihood of providing the insights needed for moving forward. There are five elements that create the right environment for healthy discovery:

1. Prepare to listen and learn

2. Conduct listening sessions from top to bottom

3. Gather relevant data

4. Synthesize the inputs

5. Present the findings to senior management

1. Prepare to learn and listen

Set a strong leadership tone to establish an attitude of being prepared to learn. As a leader, you can make a conscious decision to choose to be open and listen deeply. A powerful step is to tell your team that for the time being you are going to set aside your normal decision-making and direction-setting roles so that you can listen to other perspectives with no judgment. This is also a great time to bring a trusted adviser into the organization to help with the discovery and learning. This person may be a colleague, consultant, or board member. The critical characteristic of this person is that they need to be an independent thinker and willing to share their observations with you openly and honestly. It would be ideal if this outsider has perspectives that may challenge your own thinking.

2. Conduct listening sessions from top to bottom

I prefer to conduct sessions with a wide range of people throughout the organization. It doesn't need to be a large number of people, but it needs to be a broad range. These sessions can be fairly unstructured, and an open dialogue is encouraged. One exercise is to have each participant take a piece of paper and give them five quiet minutes. Instruct them to create a list of what is working in the company and a second list of what isn't. Have each of them read their list and capture their thoughts on a whiteboard with two separate lists: working and not working. The last step is to guide the group through a process of selecting the top 10 issues to fix, and the top 10 things that are working and should be retained. While the final list is helpful, the real benefit of this process is the insights that you'll get from the dialogue between the participants.

3. Gather relevant data

Armed with the anecdotal evidence from the listening sessions, the next step is to gather factual evidence surrounding the key areas that aren't working. It's common during the listening sessions to hear people say "a lot." The purpose of this step is to put the numbers to the issue. For example, if one of the top issues is poor on-time delivery, gather the data on orders shipped, orders taken, and production levels. This will help clarify where the issue may exist. One of my clients was struggling with on-time delivery, and the conventional wisdom was that the factory was underperforming and not producing enough. What the data showed was that the factory was producing at record levels. This issue was that orders were being loaded into the schedule without any regard for the capacity of the plant. The data helped to point the leadership team to the underlying issue of the scheduling system.

4. Synthesize the inputs

After you've conducted a number of listening sessions and gathered the essential data, it's time to boil it down to some core themes. This is hard work, and at this stage it's pretty common to be on sensory overload. Every factory, even the best ones out there, will have a long list of issues and areas for improvement. This is where you need to apply judgment and wisdom to sort through all of the muck and say: "Here's what is going on. There's a lot of noise, but these one, two, or three items are at the heart of the matter." Here are examples of typical summary statements:

- On-time delivery has suffered because production was not meeting targets for several weeks. As they got further behind, the number of expedites increased, leading to more setups and thus eroding capacity further.

- In the last 12 months, we have lost a half-dozen long-tenured employees who knew the product requirements through experience, and that wisdom did not get transferred to the new employees. This has led to the quality issues that we're experiencing.

- As part of our implementation of Lean, we dramatically reduced inventories in some key areas, and we are no longer able to absorb some real-life issues, such as machine downtime and spikes in orders.

- Orders have been much stronger than expected, exceeding production capacity. As this was occurring, we continued to offer the same historical lead time, even though we were falling further behind each week.

You may notice that the statements above do not offer solutions and that is intentional. We need to resist the urge to jump into solutions, if only for a time, to make sure that we have clarity about the problem statement. As we get further into the Fix-A-Factory process, this problem statement will serve as an anchor and help to guide us in the selection and prioritization of the actions to be implemented.

5. Present the findings to senior leadership

The final step for Revealing the Issues is to share the findings with the senior leadership team. It's important for the entire leadership team to hear the message together. My experience is that these sessions can be tense, but in the end, there is a sense of calm and resolve. Sometimes the leaders will say out loud, "Okay, that's not good news, but now we know what we're facing and we can get after it."

This session can head down two paths that need to be avoided. One path is the blaming path. Some individuals may be looking for a person to blame. I try to redirect this line of questioning, suggesting that there will be plenty of time down the road to do the postmortem. For now, it's important to be focused on working out of the situation.

The second path to be avoided happens when senior leadership dives into a problem-solving mode. I will remind them that it's best to let their teams develop the corrective action plans because they are closer to the action. I'll work with them to make sure that solid plans are created, and I'll bring that back to the senior leadership team. As you can imagine, this group can be impatient about wanting to get some actions moving, which means that it's important to get through the next stages of the Fix-A-Factory process quickly.

I'd like to conclude this meeting with a preview of what is coming next—the Reset Expectations phase, which I'll discuss in detail in the next chapter.

Case Study: Revealing the Issues

Acme Widgets is a contract manufacturer serving a wide range of manufacturing customers. They make excellent, high-precision products used in a number of high-tech industries that require absolute precision. When I was called to work with them, lead times to customers had begun to extend and on-time deliveries were worsening.

The CEO did a great job of setting the tone. He pulled together the team at the affected plant and told them that he recognized that some things weren't working. He explained that it was not a witch hunt to assign blame, but rather that they've brought in a consultant to get a fresh set of eyes on the problem. He encouraged the team to be open and honest.

I set out to listen and learn. I met with a number of people at the plant and asked for their thoughts on what was working and what wasn't. I talked to people on the floor, supervisors, schedulers, buyers, site leaders, engineers, and salespeople. At first, they were a bit hesitant to share, since some of their concerns pointed to members of the senior leadership team. Over time, as they learned that there were no negative side effects from being open, they started sharing more candidly.

Also, as part of the learning process, I participated in a number of the normal routines of the business. This included scheduling meetings and daily stand-up meetings.

Participation in the normal routines can be very insightful for understanding how things *really* work.

The learning and listening phase felt messy and chaotic. Tensions were running high, and conversations often included a heavy dose of venting, blaming, and personal attacks. Opinions of the issues ran the gamut, with operations people blaming sales, sales blaming operations, and everyone blaming leadership.

During the listening and learning process, I need to remind myself to be very disciplined to not move into the solving phase too early. I'll often get asked by people, "So, what are you seeing?" and as much as I want to answer, I deferred, saying "At this stage, I'm just getting a lot of perspectives. It's too early to draw conclusions."

As the listening and learning phase came to an end, patterns began to emerge. While there were a number of tangential issues, I felt that there were two underlying issues:

1. Dates were being promised to customers that were disconnected from the reality on the shop floor.

2. The plant was missing its production goals a little bit each day. On any given day this wasn't a big problem, but over the course of weeks and months, it had grown into a significant backlog.

The next step was to gather data to see if my hypotheses held water. The people with an analytical bias reading this will probably cringe at this approach, suggesting that the data should point to a solution and doing limited analytics to validate a hypothesis isn't good scientific problem-solving. I agree with the academic argument, but the reality is that it takes business judgment and wisdom to point the company's limited analytical resources in a direction. Just doing a raw data-up analysis is extremely time consuming and expensive, and in situations like Acme's time is at a premium.

Working with a talented data analyst, we extracted data about production levels, plant loading and scheduling, customer promise dates, and backlogs. The data told the story pretty clearly. Customers were being promised deliveries based on a standard lead time of eight weeks, but the factory had twelve weeks of backlog. This environment led to a very high rate of expediting as the factory tried to accommodate whichever customer was screaming the loudest. The high rate of expediting led to excessive changeovers, thus reducing capacity and exacerbating the problem.

The direction became self-evident. Acme needed to reset expectations for delivery dates with customers, reduce the chaos of expediting, and begin to increase throughput to reduce the lead time to normal levels.

The findings were shared with the senior leadership team. Once this direction was exposed it seemed obvious, but it was not obvious three weeks prior. Three weeks earlier, the environment was full of noise and confusion. Now we had a direction, and the senior leadership team was aligned towards getting there.

RESET EXPECTATIONS

Now you have clarity about the issues and you've defined the problem. The issues have been revealed to senior leadership, and they are aligned and supportive. You and the senior leadership team may be feeling a small ray of enthusiasm because you have clarity about the problems to be solved, but there are many other stakeholders who aren't sharing that hope yet. Customers are still frustrated. Shop floor workers are fatigued and deflated, and these sentiments may extend to suppliers and the sales force.

Before diving headlong into making changes and driving improvements, we need to get people realigned and balanced. Almost every athletic endeavor requires balance. Golfers must have an athletic, balanced stance that allows them to swing with speed and accuracy. Football linemen must have balance and strength in order to block or tackle effectively. My oldest son has his black belt in karate, and much of the training is on body position and balance. Our workforce is composed of industrial athletes and they also need balance. They need to be rested and emotionally centered.

If the factory has struggled for a long period of time, it's entirely possible that people are not in a good frame of mind. It's common to hear expressions of anger, frustration, and even depression. We're not going to win with people in that mindset. Likewise, customers may have started to lose confidence as well.

We need to provide some hope, and to do this we're going to open up, be vulnerable, and hit the reset button. Resetting expectations will help get everyone grounded, balanced, and stable, and that provides the platform for turning the tide and getting back on the path to winning.

Reset Expectations: The Stall

The process of resetting expectations has a lot in common with the actions that pilots must take when an airplane is struggling and stalls. When a factory is struggling, sometimes leadership responds by pushing harder and applying more pressure. This feels natural and right, but it can lead to a death spiral.

It is similar to a plane that needs to gain altitude. The right way to gain altitude is to apply more throttle so that there is more airflow over the wings. The increased airflow lifts the plane higher. Inexperienced pilots can make the mistake of pulling back on the yoke to gain altitude. That feels right. You want to go higher, so you point the nose where you want it to go—up! Unfortunately, this only feels good for a brief period of time. The plane lifts higher in the short term, but it also slows it down. The reduced speed reduces the airflow over the wing, creating less lift, and the plane loses altitude. The pilot responds by pulling back on the yoke further, and again there is a short lift up, but then it drops. This yo-yo of short-term lift followed by a loss of altitude and a loss of speed continues until the plane is going so slow that it reaches its stall speed. A stall in an airplane doesn't mean that the engine stalled. It means that there is not enough air flowing over the wings to overcome the force of gravity. When this happens, the plane just starts to drop. It's no longer a plane that is flying; it's a rock falling from the sky. It is in a death spiral.

With enough altitude, a stall can be corrected. The process is counterintuitive, which is why pilots train for this scenario. The pilot needs to point the nose towards the ground. Yes, that's right—*towards* the *ground*. Doing this starts to get air flowing back over the wings, and once there is enough air flowing, the wings generate lift and the plane starts flying instead of falling like a rock. At this point, the pilot can start to pull back on the yoke to gently level it out and get back to the business of safely reaching his destination (and cleaning his pants).

We need to take similar actions in the factory. Some of the things we need to do may seem counterintuitive, but it will get air flowing over the wings again.

Reset Expectations: Why Bother

The primary reason for resetting expectations is the psychological benefit. It is an awful feeling to be held to a standard that you know full well you have no chance of meeting. Having a target of 98 percent on-time delivery might be a noble aspiration when things are going well, but if things have gone awry and you're two or three weeks behind your schedule, there is zero chance of hitting that goal. It's demoralizing.

One summer, when I finished my freshman year of college, I worked for a landscaping crew. The landscaping company had two crews but only one Bobcat. I would always get assigned to the crew with no Bobcat because I was going to be the human Bobcat. In fact, "Bobcat" became my nickname for the summer. (My other nickname was "Fury," but it's best if we leave the story behind that name out of print.)

One of my most vivid recollections is a job where we had to move a lot of sand and dirt to fill in a low level on the lot. I don't remember how many yards of material needed to be moved, but it was enough to take me a week of shoveling and wheelbarrowing to move it.

The work was bad enough. It was backbreaking and hot, but I was young and strong. What broke my spirit was that it seemed it would never end. As soon as the pile started to shrink, another delivery of sand and dirt would arrive. It was completely demoralizing. At the end of the day, not only was I physically exhausted, but I was also emotionally drained. I didn't want to even contemplate going to work the next day.

When the factory is struggling, it can feel the same way. It can seem as if there are no victories because the pile never ends and the pressure from sales, customers, and executives feels constant. In order to get people energized and ready to rise to the challenge, they need to see hope, and the reset of expectations accomplishes that goal. It enables leadership to go to their teams and say, "Here's the pile of dirt we need to move today. If we get that done, then we've had a great day and we can celebrate. Forget the rest of the piles, those are for another day. Let's just move this pile and we can go home." It breaks the big pile of never-ending dirt into a series of little, surmountable mounds.

Resetting Expectations: The 4 Major Resets

If your factory is having difficulty living up to customer expectations, resetting expectations is delicate but essential. You may need to reconsider:

- Customer due dates

- Production scheduling

- Staffing and overtime

- Performance metrics

Note: These are the resets that will be needed if a factory has fallen behind and on-time delivery has tanked. I chose this scenario because it is the predominant issue that I'm seeing at the time of this writing.

Customer due dates

When production is struggling, it is common to start missing customer due dates. At first, the late shipments will be infrequent and the delay will be short. Over time, however, the deficit continues to build and real lead times creep up while on-time shipments slide.

Once a factory gets behind, it is very difficult to catch up. Let's look at a simple example: Factory XYZ typically makes 100 widgets per week and that has kept up with demand. But lately, that output has dropped to 90 widgets per week. At first, this discrepancy seems minor and goes unnoticed, but over time deliveries start to suffer. By the time the alarm bell has sounded, this shortfall had been going on for 10 weeks. The math is straightforward: 10 weeks at a deficit of 10 units per week means that the factory has fallen one week behind, or about 100 units. That means the factory is roughly one week behind.

In order to correct the situation and eat into that backlog, the factory will need to produce *above* the rate that orders are coming in. Remember, the factory has been under-producing by 10 widgets, and in order to eat into the backlog it must produce more than the incoming order flow. If the company wants the backlog returned to normal levels over the next 10 weeks, it must produce 110 widgets per week. That's a 20 percent increase over the current production levels.

I'd like to say that this example is extreme, but it isn't. I have consulted with companies that were accustomed to a 4-week lead time, and that lead time ballooned to 20 weeks due to a combination of low production throughput and surprisingly high demand. A company in this situation either needs to make major investments in people and equipment, or they need to accept that it will take a very long time to reduce lead times to normal levels.

When production output has struggled and backlog has grown, you need to come clean with your customers. That means calling the customer and giving them new delivery dates based on the realistic production rates in the factory. There is no question that this can lead to difficult conversations with customers, and some may even cancel their orders. But it is better to be up-front with them than to disappoint them down the road. Most customers will appreciate the candor because it helps them take proactive action, even if that action means moving business away from you. By being up-front, you earn a shot at winning their business back another day.

Resetting due dates gets everyone recalibrated. From the customer's perspective, they can adjust their business based on the reality of when they will receive your goods. Setting revised delivery dates often leads to robust conversations about the real priorities of the customer, and often these priorities can be accommodated. From an internal perspective, employees now have realistic dates they can strive to hit.

My recommendation is to be very conservative with the new due dates. Give yourself some wiggle room. You don't want to find yourself missing the revised due dates. The customer won't like the first reset, but it if happens a second time they will be livid.

Production and scheduling

When backlogs are on the rise, production scheduling can spiral out of control. It is common for customer service to commit to due dates that are unrealistic given the mismatch between order intake rates and production rates. This is not a malicious intent. It is just that the gap hasn't been exposed yet. This often happens in factories that don't have robust sales and operations planning processes. When the shop schedule is loaded with more than it can actually produce, excessive work orders and job orders get issued to the floor. This becomes a source of confusion as workers try to understand the real priorities amid the piles of orders in front of them. It also creates confusion in the supply chain, as purchasing people and suppliers try to understand priorities.

When the factory becomes chaotic, more manual interventions get introduced. We tend to disregard the official schedule and to manage off emails and expedite messages. Trying to keep track of emails and "hot lists" becomes the norm rather than the exception. This is a time-consuming and ineffective practice.

One of the biggest elements of achieving stability is to get out of the off-line, expediting realm and get back to trusting your information systems. Once customer expectations have been addressed and new delivery dates have been established, it's time to get the scheduling system back in order.

Every system is a little different, but the fundamentals are the same. The key is to make sure that the scheduled dates in the system match the reality of commitments to customers and excess paperwork has been removed from the floor. Expediting needs to be driven to a minimum, and the shop needs to know that they can trust the schedule that has been given to them.

Resetting the production schedule can be very challenging. It will stretch the knowledge and skills of the people that know how to work with the Enterprise Resource Planning (ERP) system. It often requires a team of people comprised of supervisors, schedulers, planners, and IT resources to craft a plan to get the production schedule back in order. I have seen some companies implement with a big bang, where they come in during the weekend, pull all the old schedules, and issue new ones. I've seen other companies implement a phased approach where they let the current job orders work their way through the system, but they meter in the new orders in line with the capacity of the plant. Both approaches can work and you'll need to decide which approach is best for your organization.

Staffing and overtime

In the early stages of falling behind, overtime can provide a surface-level appearance that all is well. However, over the course of weeks or months, overtime becomes less effective. People get tired. They don't want to give up their weekends. They also get physically and emotionally fatigued.

When we rely on overtime for extended periods, the value diminishes despite the fact that the leadership team feels obligated to continue with the overtime. I have found this fear to be unfounded. Overtime is only effective in short bursts. If you've been working more than 10 percent overtime in any area, it's time to dial it back and address the need for throughput by fixing the underlying issues and increasing staffing.

Staffing is another factor that needs to be considered. If the factory has fallen behind and the backlog has grown, it is entirely possible that the workforce may need to grow. This is a very delicate proposition. Leadership must consider what will happen when the backlog has been reduced and the situation has returned to a normal steady state. How will the newly hired people be treated? At the time of this writing, the unemployment rate is quite low and hiring is very difficult. Creativity may be needed to find quality people to bring into the organization.

A final consideration is retention. When a factory devolves into chaos, the workforce can become very frustrated. Nobody wants to work in a chaotic environment where they don't have the materials and tools to do their job. There will be some people that will decide that it isn't worth it and choose to look elsewhere.

The workforce needs to be handled strategically. There is a finite supply of workers available and the ones that you already employ have choices. You need to treat your workers as if they are family and show them the respect they deserve. They didn't get you into this predicament, but you're going to need them to get out of it.

Performance metrics

Metrics that are perpetually off target are demoralizing and counterproductive. The leadership team must ask the question, "Given our current situation, what does good look like?" The metrics should inform leaders as to whether the situation is improving or continuing to degrade. It does no good to have a metric that is a completely unachievable goal.

Let's take the example of on-time delivery. Perhaps you've had a history of delivering 96 percent on time, and you've set a target for the year of 98 percent. However, due to challenges in the factory, on-time delivery has dropped to 75 percent. The current goal of 98 percent is unrealistic. A target that is this disconnected from reality serves no positive purpose. In order to reset this metric, the leadership team may say, "We're going to reset customer due dates in three weeks, and after that I'd expect to see an immediate bump in on-time delivery. I'd consider it a success if we were back at 90 percent in three weeks, and then a steady climb to 96 percent within three months. Once we reach that level, we can start thinking about the 98 percent target again."

Recalibrating the definition of success will create small victories and give your workers something to strive for. In contrast, if the metrics aren't recalibrated, workers will become numb and demoralized.

There is one bit of nuance related to communication of performance against the new targets. I've experienced situations where the leader congratulates the workforce for an achievement of the new targets, but then he can't stop himself from saying "but." He'll say: "It's great that you hit yesterday's on-time delivery target of 88 percent, *but* customers are still unhappy." That "but" isn't helpful. The team needs to celebrate the victory of hitting yesterday's goals and be energized to do a little bit better the next day with no ifs, ands, or buts. Qualifying every victory with a "but" will leave workers demoralized. That isn't the way to turn the ship around.

Reset performance expectations based on the reality of the current situation and celebrate progress towards your goals.

Reset Expectations: Wrap-up

Resetting expectations is the second phase of the process for fixing a factory. Getting recalibrated doesn't fix the situation, but it has a tremendous psychological impact. It tells everyone "What is done is done. The past can't be undone, but let's look to the future."

During the reset, leadership needs to set a tone of confidence coupled with humility, honesty, and vulnerability. There needs to be an acknowledgment of the reality of the situation married to a stubborn resolution that we'll get through it. This is all done with a calm and empathetic tone.

PRIORITIZE THE CORE 10

Now that the expectations have been reset, it's time to put the wheels in motion to fix the underlying issues. All factories have a set of core systems that must be operating with reasonable proficiency for the factory as a whole to have good outcomes. When a factory becomes distressed, it is usually due to weakness in one or more of these core systems.

In this chapter, we'll cover the systems that I most commonly see as the causes of factories in distress. I openly acknowledge that this is not a comprehensive list of every system in a factory, and some may argue that I've missed a core system. I welcome that feedback and look forward to the discussion and dialogue. This is a living list that may be changed from time to time as manufacturers and the business climate change.

The Core 10 Systems are:

1. Talent System

2. Clean and Safe Factory System

3. Management System

4. Equipment Reliability System

5. Quality System

6. Supply

7. Inventory

8. Sales and Operations Planning

9. Data and Measurement

10. Operating System

You may notice that my wording is a little different than many textbooks. I intentionally tried to remove the jargon. These are factory fundamentals, and you can be fundamentally strong in each of these areas without implementing the techniques that can move you from competence to excellence. For example, you can have a clean and well-organized factory without embracing the 5S methodology of Lean. I toured one of my clients through another shop and the first thing they said was, "This factory is so clean." My response was simply, "Yes, it is. They are thinking about starting to implement Lean this year." Clean and safe factories existed long before Lean concepts and language hit the shores of the U.S.

I have no issues with Lean. If that is the operations model that you're embracing, then use those tools, techniques, and philosophies. My point is that you don't need to be fully committed to a Lean Transformation in order to reach a level of health and good performance in each of these core systems.

With that, let's explore each of these systems.

Core #1: Talent System

The worker shortage has been widely reported for the past few years. This is a real phenomenon that is impacting the ability of companies to grow and produce a quality product cost effectively.

A mid-size metal fabrication company was having difficulty hitting daily production targets. They implemented Lean techniques, including standard work and hour-by-hour charts, but to no avail. When those techniques didn't work, they started swapping out supervisors because that certainly had to be the problem. Again, no improvement. They finally looked at employee turnover and a major problem became very apparent. Over the last several years, they had cycled through six people for every increase in headcount. This had created a vicious cycle where new employees weren't trained because "they aren't going to stick around anyway," and the employees left because "we weren't trained and we were treated like shit from day one." It became clear that this was a core issue that needed addressing and the company set out to improve its talent system.

When I enter a factory that is struggling and I'm in the Reveal the Issues stage, the talent situation is one of the first places that I start because it has become such a pervasive issue. In order to understand the health of the talent system, I'll ask questions like:

- What percent of the workforce has been here less than one year? Two years, five years, ten years?

- How have those numbers changed over the last few years?

- How many experienced workers have retired or quit over the last few years?

- What is the yield from the hiring process? I.e., how many people need to be hired in order to net an employee that stays for one year or more?

Early in my career, companies that had a reputation for good pay and benefits had a line of applicants waiting for a job. When an opening popped up, HR could open up the file drawer, look for a good fit, make a call, and the job was filled. Often, those employees would stay for years and even decades because they were grateful to have a good job. Those days are gone and I don't see them returning in the near future. Employees hold the cards today. They can choose from many jobs and employers, and if they don't like the way they are being treated they'll go somewhere else.

Innovative manufacturers are trying a variety of approaches to address the situation. Some have created internal development programs. Others have partnered with a local vocational college. Others still have started to increase pay and benefits or even reduce hiring standards. These changes often happen when companies have their back against the wall and they need some workers immediately. These are ad hoc solutions targeted at getting an immediate resolution to a staffing shortage and at best they experience mixed success. These ad hoc approaches, coupled with lukewarm results, often lead to a blame game. The operations team blames HR and the temp agencies for not finding good people, and HR blames operations for not onboarding people properly and creating a positive culture.

The underlying issue is companies are still viewing hiring as a tactical, administrative process. They are applying a staffing approach that worked for decades but doesn't work any longer. Talent needs to be elevated to a more strategic level, almost on a level footing with customers, because the competition for employees is every bit as intense as the competition for customers.

There are five components of the talent system that warrant brief exploration because each of these components must be strong to uphold the entire talent system. They are:

- Talent brand

- Talent pipeline

- Screening and hiring process

- Onboarding process

- Training and development process

These items are focused on attracting, hiring, and getting people through the first year of employment. There are many other factors that also need consideration, including culture, training and development, job security, compensation, and safety. However, for the purpose of this book, I'll focus on these five elements.

Talent brand

When we think of "brand," we often think of a company's logo and colors, but brand is much more than that. It represents what comes to mind when people think of your company. It is your reputation. Companies work diligently to have a strong brand in the marketplace. It may be a brand based on technical innovation, elegant design, low prices, or operational excellence. While this kind of branding shapes the reputation of the company among the customer community, what about the reputation of the company in the community from which you are trying to recruit?

All companies have a reputation. In some cases it's positive and in other cases it isn't. Consider these well-known companies and the reputations that they have earned:

- Walmart: low wages

- Google: eclectic nerd heaven

- Any hedge fund: greedy, money-ruled, workaholic

- IBM: blue suits, stiff, and formal (I know that's an outdated view, but it's still what I think of)

- Amazon: meat grinder

- Apple Stores: young, hip

- US Post Office: crabby bureaucrats

What is *your* employment brand? What do you want your target population of employees to think about when they hear your company's name? How are you going to be different from other companies targeting the same population? Do you pay better? Is it a fun environment? Do you believe in flexibility? Are you an amiable company, or are you driven to win? Do you develop careers and promote from within? Just as with product marketing, you can't be all things to all people, and you'll need to focus your efforts and dollars. A shotgun approach that tries to reach everyone fails because the message is fragmented. Just as a consumer will search for the lowest price for a commodity, so too will potential employees search for the highest wages if they are comparing one generic employer against another.

Some larger companies are getting very good at cultivating an employment brand, but I find it rare in mid-market companies. I encourage you to go to Indeed.com or another hiring site and do a job search for one of the positions in your factory. I searched for welders in St. Paul, Minnesota, and this is the beginning of the first listing that came up:

Summary

The primary role for this position is to operate fabricating machines such as cutoff saws, shears and brakes that cut, shape, and bend metal sheets and structures to manufacture XXXX.

Essential Functions

- *Performs a variety of tasks involving strenuous manual labor; performs manual work.*

- *Utilizes all hand tools and grinders.*

- *Develops layout and plans sequence of operations.*

- *Locates and marks bending and cutting lines onto workpiece.*

- *Positions, aligns, fits, and welds together parts.*

- *Fabricates and assembles sheet metal products.*

You learn nothing about the company or what it stands for in this listing. A reader could easily draw the conclusion that this company views its workers as nothing more than laborers. Contrast that posting with this one, which I found after a little digging.

For more than 70 years, Acme Products has been satisfying customers' most demanding requirements with durable, precision plastic products. Our companies create customized equipment solutions for manufacturing plants, laboratories and lead the industry in plastic distribution and tight-tolerance machining.

We are currently hiring for our Apprentice Welder/Fabricator program. Learn how to weld and fabricate plastic components from industry experts. This two-year structured program will set you up for success in a highly specialized field. Earn raises at multiple milestones. The starting wage is $xx.00/hour with an additional .50 *increase after 6 months. This is a full-time direct hire position with benefits to start. We offer a very stable working environment with consistent hours—Monday through Friday, 7AM–3:30PM.*

This posting implies several things about the employer:

1. They are willing to invest in your training and development to help you build your career.

2. They value you enough that they won't make you go through a temp agency.

3. They consider stability and work-life balance important.

4. They are proud to make high-precision parts.

This employer has considered their employment brand and they've integrated it into their job posting, targeting a specific demographic and psychographic profile.

Having clarity about the reputation that you want in the marketplace and walking the talk of that brand message are key steps for developing a healthy and stable workforce. Armed with clarity about your employment brand, it's time to evaluate the pipeline of people.

Pipeline

The term talent pipeline is shorthand for describing the target population from which you want to hire and the tactics that you'll use to attract them to your organization.

Some examples of talent pipelines include:

Target	Sample Tactic
Military veterans	Partnership with a local veterans' placement organization
Vocational school graduates	Participation in job fairs at the school
Specific immigrant community	Postings at the local community center in the native language
Workers currently employed at a nearby factory	Referral bonus to current employees
High school students	Participation in job fairs and hosting tours on Manufacturing Day.
Current employees	Internal schools

The options are limited only by your imagination. The key point is that you will need to pick a strategy and execute it with rigor, dedication, and persistence. Pipelines take time to mature because communities want to know that you're committed. The world has become a skeptical and distrustful place, and you should expect that you won't be greeted warmly at the outset. Your trust will need to be earned. However, as with any change, there are a few early adopters. So, when you start putting up flyers at the veterans center, you might get a small expression of interest, but the vast majority of people will sit back and watch to see what happens. If there is good feedback from the early adopters, then others will join in and momentum will be established.

I want to make a special comment about temp agencies. Many mid-market companies have turned to temp agencies to solve their staffing challenges. The reasoning is that the temp agencies have access to more people through a broader network. In addition, temp agencies remove some of the risk of hiring because an employee that isn't panning out can be terminated easily.

I think temp agencies are a fine solution if there are short-term needs. Ideally, the temp agency can help you ramp up and ramp down quickly. That said, I have a bias against the use of temp agencies in temp-to-hire models for four reasons:

1. The management of the workforce is strategic and not transactional, and the company should keep strategic activities inside the company. Developing a robust talent pipeline can become a distinctive competency.

2. Temp agencies will not be able to tell your brand story as well as you can. Temp agencies represent many employers. Therefore, they will not be as committed to selling your story as you are.

3. I do not believe you will attract the best workers if you use a temp agency. Top workers are not going to be willing to go through a three- to six-month trial period as a temp worker just to see if they'll make it.

4. Having a significant population of temps can create a class system in the factory. They have different compensation

and different benefits, and they are treated differently. I hear things like, "They aren't a real employee yet" and they are treated as such. A company facing a short-term workforce reduction will have no qualms with letting the temps go as if they aren't real people with real lives. Temps are treated as second-class citizens and that makes it very difficult to have a fully engaged and aligned workforce.

People on the Autism Spectrum in the Workforce

I'd like to make a case for the population of people with autism. This group of specially enabled people are an untapped gold mine of talent. According to the National Autism Association, 1 in 59 children have autism—my son being one of them. With 320 million people in the U.S., and 36 percent of those between 18 and 44 (2010 US Census), we can deduce that there are nearly 2 million people in prime working age on the autism spectrum.

People on the autism spectrum can be excellent workers. They are often highly intelligent and they seek the regular patterns that are typical in many workplaces.

This population will need support. It is common for people on the spectrum to struggle with social and verbal communication skills. Also, it is a spectrum disorder, meaning that it ranges in severity. However, with a bit of special attention and training, this is a wonderfully talented, dedicated, and loyal population.

> Progressive, high-tech companies like Microsoft have created autism hiring centers for the sole purpose of tapping into the special gifts of this population.

With a strong employment brand and a pipeline of potential employees, it's time to move to the hiring process.

Screening and hiring

The screening and hiring process has two goals that may conflict with each other. One goal is to vet the candidate enough to ensure a high degree of confidence in her success. This includes thorough interviews at multiple levels that probe into the candidate's history, assessing technical skills, checking for a values match, and performing reference checks, background checks, and drug screens. The second goal of the process is to leave a positive impression with the candidate and sell them on the opportunity. The screening and hiring process will be the first time that the candidate has interacted with the company, and the candidate is likely to assume that the way he is treated during the screening and hiring processes is a lens into how he'll be treated as an employee.

Today's workforce can be impatient when waiting for responses. They expect the hiring process to be quick, decisive, and user-friendly. If your process is cumbersome, slow, and bureaucratic, you will lose good candidates. However, if it is streamlined too much and critical filters are removed, the company will hire unsuitable candidates.

As much as we'd like to have an ideal process that is fast, friendly, and thorough, the reality is that it involves trade-offs. For example, the more interviews that are required to vet a candidate, the harder they will be to schedule and the longer they will take. The extra time that the candidate must invest will not be viewed favorably. As long as the situation remains, recruits hold the power and employers will be pressed to find solutions that help to ensure that they get the best candidates.

The good news is that the bar is set quite low at many manufacturers and little adjustments can set you apart. I was working with a client who specializes in metal fabrication and they were struggling to fill their welding openings. They adjusted to accommodate same-day interviews of welding candidates and within weeks all of the openings were filled.

Onboarding

Onboarding is the initial time that a new employee spends with a company. The time frame starts on their first day of work and may extend up to one year.

The first few days of employment really sets the tone with a worker. They are drinking in what they are seeing and developing a sense for whether they have made the right decision.

I've personally had both great and horrible onboarding experiences. On the bad side, one company started my career as a senior executive by putting me in a small conference room (my office wasn't ready) with no phone or computer. No introductions were made, no nothing. Just the HR forms. That was it. The implied message was "you're a big boy, go figure it out." By contrast, another company was fully prepared for my first day. I was greeted in the lobby and shown to my office, which had a flower arrangement welcoming my wife and me to the company. I was given my badge and then we walked around the plant for introductions. My calendar was prepopulated with important meetings, and I was given instruction on where to find key information. The company had also arranged for someone to take me to lunch each day. The first company had me shaking my head at the disorganization. The second company had me telling my wife that the company is a real class act.

In a robust and efficient factory, new workers will need to be fully capable when they enter the production environment. They will need to know the work procedures and quality requirements. For most companies, this will necessitate a more thorough training program.

The onboarding program must also account for the social and team needs of the employee. New employees need to feel welcome and part of the team, which means that they will need support. Existing employees have a key role to play here.

In the old days, there was often a trial-by-fire approach for new employees. They were "thrown to the wolves" and if they survived, they were considered tough enough to stay. It was a borderline hazing ritual. Those days are long gone, thank goodness, and employers need to embrace the challenges faced by new workers and help them reach their full capabilities.

One simple analysis is to review the number of people who stayed with the company for over one year after they were hired. If this number is low, it may be an indicator of an onboarding process that needs improvement. There could be other causes as well, such as inadequate screening (e.g., hiring people who have a history of attendance issues).

Talent system: Wrap-up

The talent system is number one on our list of core systems because it is critical to success and is failing in many companies. Most manufacturers are struggling to hire, develop, and retain the workforce they need to meet their goals. External forces are blamed: The new generation doesn't want to work, the school system pushes people to college, and there is a stigma against manufacturing. While there may be truth in all of it, grousing does not change the reality. We have evolved from the early days of the Industrial Revolution, where workers were leaving the farm in search of a better life for their family. Today's workforce has choices. They demand good pay, a great culture, and expect to be seen and treated as individuals.

Developing a strong talent system is a company issue, not just an HR issue. In the short term, tourniquets may be required to get through the immediate situation, but for the longterm health of your talent base, it is time to elevate workforce development as a strategic issue at the executive level.

Core #2: Clean and Safe Factory System

The condition of the factory is a reflection of the leadership's biases and attitudes. A dirty or unsafe factory may represent a lack of respect for the workforce, a disregard for rigor and discipline, or a bias against people doing anything other than cranking out more parts. I've been in hundreds of factories and I've never seen a high-performance plant that is a mess. That said, being clean and safe doesn't automatically mean that the factory is high performance. Having a clean and safe factory sets the tone for the workplace. It says to employees, "We care about our people. We are professionals. We're disciplined, and we do the right thing."

While there are differences between having a clean factory and having a safe factory, I've lumped them together in this section because they are related to the work environment—both the physical workspace and the behaviors and habits of people.

Creating a clean and safe factory isn't complicated. It doesn't require a lot of training or extensive investments in technology. It simply demands the desire and discipline to make it a reality. I understand that there are a large number of compliance-oriented technical specifications, but that isn't what I'm talking about. I'm referring to behaviors. Do people behave safely every day? Do they keep their work areas clean? Does leadership make good decisions about safety, such as shutting down a process when an unsafe situation arises? Does leadership allow time for cleaning and do they make sure that the cleaning is happening? Do people have their eyes open to safety issues or do they walk past them every day and assume that is the way it is? Once there is a foundation of solid, safe behaviors, engagement with an environmental health and safety professional can help take safety to the next level and ensure that the factory is compliant with codes and regulations.

I've seen environments where people walk on snow-covered pipes 20 feet in the air on semi-trailers as if it were normal and safe. I've seen people in open-toed shoes carrying sheets of glass. I've been in buildings where you didn't dare touch anything for fear of ruining your clothes. Don't get me started on the bathrooms that make outhouses a preferred option.

When I encounter a dirty and dangerous factory, I know that I have my work cut out for me because there is something amiss at the leadership level. I don't expect perfection. I'm only looking for the egregious disregard of cleanliness and safety. We need to get to the root of this issue because the leadership traits that are creating this environment will exist in other core systems.

There are always excuses about why a factory is dirty and dangerous. "It's the nature of our industry," or "If people use common sense, they won't get hurt." These are deflections. The reason that the factory is dirty and dangerous is because of leadership. As leaders, we get the behavior we tolerate. If there are people who are engaging in risky behaviors and people who aren't keeping their areas clean, it's because leadership tolerates it. On one consulting engagement, the CEO asked me to give him a tour. I walked through the factory with him, giving him time to talk to workers. We were almost done with the tour when I realized that he wasn't wearing the proper personal protective equipment. What kind of message do you think that sent to the workforce? Here was the CEO not paying attention to safety and I tolerated it. It was shameful. The CEO and I discussed this, and for his next tour we both were very diligent about following the safety rules.

I'm not minimizing the effort it takes. If a factory has a history of being dirty or unsafe, it could necessitate a huge shift. There may be years of experience that have created norms of behavior that will take energy and commitment to change. Leadership will need to walk the talk. Sooner or later there will be a "Tylenol moment" that will challenge leadership to do the right thing despite potential harm to the business. "Tylenol moment" refers to a series of seven murders in Chicago in 1982. Somebody was lacing Tylenol capsules with potassium cyanide. The manufacturer, Johnson & Johnson, was quickly ruled out as the source of the issue since the poisoned pills came from different plants. Nevertheless, Johnson & Johnson had every bottle of Tylenol recalled and they offered to replace any pills that had already been purchased. This cost the company nearly $300 million (2018 dollars). They didn't need to do this. They weren't at fault, but they did it anyway because they knew that their reputation hung in the balance.

Leadership will be scrutinized much the same way that Johnson & Johnson was. When people see leaders standing up and making the hard calls, they'll see that the leadership team is serious about creating a safe and clean workplace.

A client recently faced one of these Tylenol moments. They were loading an unusually large product onto a trailer. They didn't have a method for doing it, but the team (engineers, associates, and managers) had devised a way that they thought would probably be okay if they were careful. Thankfully, there was one employee who didn't think it was safe and he took his concern up the chain until his voice was heard. Luckily, he was heard. The loading operation was stopped and a proper loading method was designed. The shipment was a day late, the trucker was irate, and considerable cost was incurred, but the associates were safe. If this situation had gone unchecked, it could have ended with people hurt. It highlights the momentum and energy that can persuade people to go along to get along. In this case, plant leadership did the right thing by thanking and recognizing the employee who showed the courage to raise the alarm.

Instilling a safe and clean factory culture requires leaders to develop the skills to drive and sustain change. These are the same skills that are needed to create strength in the other Core 10 systems, which is why this system is near the top of the list. Being strong in the process of maintaining a safe and clean environment will create good outcomes with the workforce, and it demonstrates the leadership muscle to implement and sustain fundamental systems.

Core #3: Management System

For the purpose of this book, I am referring to the management system from the plant manager down to the value-adding shop floor workers. Typically, this chain of command involves a plant manager, production manager, supervisors, and leads. The titles may change, but the structure is common. Companies with weak management systems will have difficulty implementing and sustaining most changes. The management system is the combination of having the right people, with the right skills and capabilities, armed with the right tools in the right proportion to enable the shop floor to achieve its goals.

Unfortunately, many organizations are struggling with their management systems. They don't have enough strength in the chain from leads to supervisors to production managers to effectively manage and lead the factory.

Often, the supervisors are blamed for not following through or, worse yet, they're accused of intentionally undermining the change because they are "resistant to change," "anchor draggers," or "cavemen." However, the underlying issue usually extends far beyond the individual. I've seen many factories where each supervisor is expected to cover 30 to 50 people over thousands of square feet. They spend much of their day firefighting, usually due to failures in some of the other foundational systems described in this chapter, and yet somehow they are the convenient target of blame.

Production Supervision:
Where Textbooks End and Reality Begins

Being a production supervisor is one of the most difficult and thankless jobs in a factory. I learned firsthand one summer as an intern at a GM factory in Saginaw, Michigan, where I filled in for vacationing supervisors. There I was, a 21-year-old college kid supervising a bunch of grizzled workers. It was daunting at first, but I got the hang of it and I learned how to survive.

My approach was to enter the new department I was covering and ask a couple people who really ran things on the UAW (United Automobile Workers) side. They'd point me to a couple of people and I'd go find them. I'd introduce myself and say, "I've been asked to supervise this department for a week. You and I both know that I don't know anything about this department. I'll make you a deal. I'll stay out of your way if you just keep things running this week. Just let me know if something goes crazy." I'd give him a roll of quarters to buy coffee for anyone who needed a payoff (it was the currency of the plant).

In contrast, another college kid was supervising another area and he wanted to make his mark, so he decided to be

---

a hard-ass driver. One of his machines was down one day, so he walked up to the mechanic and asked, "How long will it be before the machine is fixed?" The mechanic said, "Four hours." The kid said, "Make it two." As you can imagine, that didn't go over too well and it took three days to get fixed. The workers also subjected him to a hazing day where they played endless practical jokes on him, like replacing his three-wheeled bike hubs with pencils so that he'd crash to the floor when he got on his bike.

I had my own rough moments. I had to send a guy home for sleeping on the job. Afterwards, I asked my superintendent if I did the right thing and he said, "Sure kid. You did. Just be careful. He's going to court next week for shooting his wife."

That job was one of the biggest growth experiences of my life. Like many growth experiences it sucked a lot of the time, but I enjoyed being in the middle of the action, resolving issues, and making things happen. As a soon-to-be college senior, I went back to school battle hardened and ready to look at academia through the lens of reality.

Supervisors are the ones orchestrating the activities with the value-adding workers every day to try to achieve the goals for safety, delivery, cost, and quality. In the old days, they were called foremen and they were a tough bunch who managed to use their extensive knowledge of the area and their strong force of personality to get things done. They could sense when things weren't quite right and they'd make adjustments on the fly. They'd expedite parts, hop on a forklift, work around the issue, or cobble the machine back together. Doing the job well meant doing whatever was needed to get the job done.

Today, we expect more from our supervisors. We want them to be proactive problem-solvers and not reactive firefighters. We want them to be coaches and not tyrants. Hopping on the forklift is now a bad thing that is discouraged because we want them doing the standard work of a leader. We want them leading the implementation of continuous improvement initiatives. When there's a quality problem, we want them to conduct an 8D investigation and lead daily stand-up meetings in a way that engages their workers. They must also do standard work audits to ensure that the process is being followed.

The practice of having a supervisor cover a large territory and many people is a carryover from factories in the 20th century. In that era, one supervisor might have been able to cover 35 people (with no leads) because the people had long tenure on their jobs and the jobs were repetitive. When I was an engineer at Saginaw Steering Gear, a General Motors factory making drive shafts and steering components, there were assembly jobs that had a seven-second cycle time. In other words, the workers repeated the same operation every seven seconds. It wasn't a great work environment, but it was stable and easy to supervise. The work areas pretty much ran themselves, and the supervisor's job was to handle the administrative tasks, put out fires, and deal with the occasional disciplinary action or union grievance.

Most modern factories don't look like that General Motors plant. I see highly complicated machine setups, cycle times that can stretch over many hours, and a wide high variety of products. The changes in the workforce have compounded the challenges. As baby boomers have retired, factories are losing critical institutional knowledge. These workers knew the products and processes deeply. In many cases, this wisdom is not being captured and passed on to the next generation of workers. The knowledgeable workers that are retiring are being replaced by entry-level workers who are unfamiliar with both the products and processes of the company.

The modern factory needs more shop floor leadership than a 20th century factory. I'm sure that there are exceptions, like a highly automated plant that is operated by highly skilled technicians, but I don't see many of those. Most of the plants I see still have a lot of people who need more training, support, leadership, and management oversight than was needed before. We can use our experience in office settings as a comparison. In most office environments, a manager will start to feel overwhelmed when she gets to 10 to 12 employees. That is because they are dealing with complex work and workers who require considerable coaching and development. The modern factory environment resembles an office environment much more so than the factories of old.

Factories that don't develop a strong leadership structure encounter a number of issues:

- High involuntary turnover is seen among the supervisors and leads as management searches for the super-human person who can excel in the role with little or no training. These people are rare, and it will be unlikely that you'll find enough of them to meet all the needs of your factory. The high turnover also sends a strong message of disrespect to the workforce as they watch long-tenured, capable people get fired or demoted because they struggled to succeed in the role of lead or supervisor.

- Employees are disengaged because they do not get enough positive interaction with their leader.

- Changes and improvements are not sustained because the supervisors do not have the time to reinforce the changes. They are consumed with the urgent and have little time to dedicate to the important.

- High turnover of new employees often occurs because they feel inadequately trained and supported during the onboarding.

The needs of each company are unique, but an effective leadership structure often follows these ratios:

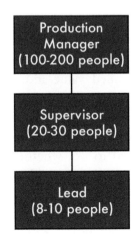

Each of these roles has similar accountabilities with the primary difference being the span of control. The key accountabilities for production leadership often include:

- Achieve goals for safety, quality, delivery, and cost

- Develop a high-performance team

- Represent the culture of the company through their actions

- Perform administrative duties (e.g., payroll)

A robust structure helps ensure that shop floor leadership has the time to take care of important but non-urgent issues, like training their team and doing standard work observations. If I see a shop that has dramatically skinnier ratios, my antennae go up because it is a likely source of some of the troubles that the factory is experiencing.

The development of highly capable leads and supervisors takes time, training, and patience. Often, these people have been placed into these positions because they were the hardest working, most dedicated, and most skilled value-adding workers in an area. Most have received little or no training and development, and they are thrust into the job and told to figure it out. With no training and a limited understanding of their duties, many resort to doing what they used to do, whether that is chasing down parts or hopping on a machine to produce parts.

Developing supervisors and leads requires a well-designed and rigorous program executed over months and years. The most effective programs that I've seen include classroom training in small chunks followed by on-the-floor coaching with direct support from supervisors. Production managers need to be coaching and reinforcing the training with their supervisors, and the supervisors need to reinforce the materials with their leads. If a factory is just getting started with the development of shop floor leadership, it needs to start at the top. They need to coach their people and they can't do that if they don't know the materials themselves. Unfortunately, I usually see the opposite approach, where development is thrust upon the leads and supervisors, but there is no support from above and, therefore, no behavioral change.

There is also an infrastructure that should be in place to support and develop the pipeline of shop floor leaders. Ideally, for each position there are two or three people who are ready to advance to the next level. This implies that training and coaching must be a continual process to support the need for new shop floor leaders, which can happen due to company growth, promotions, retirements, and separations.

Done properly, the organizational structure suggested here should pay for itself. While the accountants may view this as excessive overhead, this structure should provide a much higher degree of operational excellence. I recommend setting this as an expectation. As supervisory leverage is changed and leads are added to the structure, determine the improvements needed in productivity, quality, safety, and employee turnover to justify the cost structure that comes with this organization structure. If those goals aren't being met, it should serve as a trigger to review the effectiveness of the development program.

If the shop floor leadership structure is weak, the priorities may need to be adjusted. There is no sense in pushing changes that require the dedication and follow-through of already overloaded supervisors. The initiatives will be destined to fail. It's better to find programs that either don't require additional efforts from the supervisors or that reduce some of their workload. For example, a factory that was experiencing a high level of late deliveries from suppliers instituted a shortage management tool that didn't require the supervisors to sit at their computers and respond to emails. The key is to avoid improvement initiatives that are highly dependent on supervisor and lead diligence. If the right leadership structure doesn't exist, a push to get supervisors to put more emphasis on a particular area will be transient.

In addition to having the right structure in place, there also needs to be tools and a system for the supervisors. In Lean circles, this is referred to as leader standard work. This is the daily routine each person in the management chain of command follows to ensure that operations are performing effectively. Leader standard work helps to take the mystery out of how to be a supervisor because it provides structure and routine for the job while also allowing flexibility to respond to unforeseen issues. Leader standard work often includes:

- Key performance metrics for items such as cost, quality, delivery, and safety.

- A communication board that is used to convey information to his team.

- A series of "tier" meetings, usually one for his direct team and one for one level up.

- A daily action sheet to capture issues and corrective actions.

- A list of routine items that must be done occasionally, such as conducting an audit of a process.

- A method for capturing and implementing ideas for improvement.

A robust leader standard work system can do wonders for a company's ability to execute daily and drive sustainable, continuous improvement. When a system like this is lacking, it usually indicates a management style based on reactivity and firefighting.

Core #4: Equipment Reliability System

The existence of reliable and dependable equipment is another core system. We can't make quality products if the equipment isn't running properly. Unreliable equipment can lead to poor customer service, excessive costs, high inventories, and unsafe conditions.

Getting a good understanding of equipment reliability can be challenging. Most mid-market companies have poor data about unplanned equipment downtime. In addition to poor data, many people in factories become accustomed to equipment that is performing poorly; they just accept it as the way things are. They'll remember when a piece of equipment went down for three days, but 15 minutes here and an hour there will be discounted as unavoidable. For example, an operator may need to reset a controller four times a shift, adding up to a lost hour of production, but that is just written off as normal production.

In the absence of reasonable downtime data, I turn to other methods to understand the robustness of the equipment reliability systems.

One of my methods is to simply walk the shop floor with a supervisor or lead—someone who is familiar with the day-to-day issues on the floor. I'll ask the dumb questions to try to extract a picture of what is going on; when I do this, I try to avoid jargon as much as possible. Questions might include:

- Are there pieces of equipment that are problematic? Tell me about those.

- How do you go about taking care of the routine maintenance?

- Is there equipment that is keeping you from hitting your goals?

- What's your worst piece of equipment that you need to use routinely? Tell me about it.

- Tell me about what maintenance work the operators do and what is done by maintenance workers.

- Is there equipment that you feel is too far gone and needs to be replaced? Has it been requested? What happened with that request?

- Tell me a little about how you make time for maintenance, given that we're so far behind.

The purpose of these questions is to create a dialogue and get them talking to me. While walking the floor, I'm also using my own observations to supplement what he's saying.

Doing a few of these tours will create a directionally correct view of the condition of the systems that lead to equipment reliability. It should also leave you with an impression as to whether there are equipment reliability issues that need to be addressed immediately as part of fixing the factory. The key is to pare it down to the critical few and get an action plan in place. This may be as simple as getting some badly needed maintenance prioritized, but it may be more significant and require the purchase of a new piece of equipment or an overhaul.

The good news is that equipment reliability is rarely one of the biggest issues affecting factory performance; if it is an issue, it's often isolated. That said, I have been in factories that have allowed their equipment to deteriorate to the point of no return. It became a vicious cycle of low profitability leading to lack of upgrades and maintenance, which further eroded factory performance. Not every factory can be fixed. At some point, the factory will require a substantial capital infusion or it will continue on a path to decline and eventual closure. While this is a difficult reality to face, it is better to accept and confront it now while you're controlling the business.

Core #5: Quality System

As we work towards fixing the factory, we want to understand the impact that defects are having on the effectiveness of the factory. There are two key questions to answer:

1. What is the impact of defects that have left the factory and made it to customers?

2. What is the impact of defects captured within the factory?

These are basic questions, and you might be surprised by the number of companies that struggle to answer them. They may have a wall full of plaques and certifications like ISO 9000, ISO 13485, ISO 16949, etc., yet defects routinely make it to the customer and to the next operation. I find that the certifications have little correlation with actual performance.

A mid-market precision machine shop made parts for several high-tech industries, which have very rigorous quality system expectations But they were struggling to keep up with customer demand and on-time delivery was eroding. As we investigated the quality system, we found that even though their system complied with industry standards, it was coming at a very high cost. The factory was relying on inspections to catch defects and the defect rates were quite high.

When they started a new run, they would make a small sample and send it to the QC lab for first-article approval before beginning the production run. The QC lab work could require up to several hours and during this time the machine was idle. QC was finding defects on close to 25 percent of the submitted samples, which required changes to the program and tooling followed by a resubmittal. We quantified the hours of production that were lost to the first-article process and it was clear that it constituted a major capacity leak. Armed with this insight, we were able to work on streamlining the first-article process and we fixed some of the process issues that were leading to failed first-article checks.

Addressing all of the quality issues can seem overwhelming. I have found that focusing on the top three issues makes the solution easier to absorb and implement. For example, let's say that one of the causes of defects in a certain part is that the specification is unclear, leading to operator errors. Updating this one print is a relatively easy and quick job. However, if this was expanded to include *all* prints, the project would become enormous and there would be no progress. After months of consistently focusing on the top three, factories will find that they've made a big dent in the list of issues that are creating defects.

Core #6: Supply

Suppliers are an integral part of delivering value to customers. For many companies, they represent 30 to 70 percent of the total cost of the product. Yet, management of the supply base is usually treated as a transactional and tactical activity. I have experienced three broad categories of supplier issues that can dramatically impact the performance of the factory:

1. Misaligned value streams

2. Ineffective supply base management

3. Weak sales and operations planning

Misaligned value streams

A well-designed value stream between suppliers and the factory can align inventory positions, lead times, minimum order quantities, packaging quantities, and ordering methods so that the right product arrives on time without excess inventory.

Problems arise when there is a mismatch between the reality of how the business works and the design of the supply chain value stream. Here are a couple examples:

- An expensive part is used infrequently, so the company carries a very small inventory. Due to the low volume, the supplier doesn't carry inventory either. The lead time to get the part from the supplier is three months due to the casting that must be ordered. However, the customer expects the part in four weeks, and when they place orders, they tend to place them in large batches. This mismatch of customer expectations, order patterns, and supplier lead times will inevitably lead to stock-outs and backorders.

- The minimum order quantity for a part is four pallets, but the warehouse only has room for two pallets. Therefore, when the shipment arrives the warehouse team needs to stuff the extra pallets somewhere, often leading to lost parts and inaccurate inventory levels.

A factory can absorb an occasional misaligned value stream, but if the issue is pervasive, the factory will struggle. Every day will be a firefight of shortages, expedites, and rescheduling because the right parts will not be available at the right time to complete production.

The remedy for this situation is to get the value stream aligned. This requires a cooperative effort between operations, purchasing, and the supplier. The result is often referred to as a Plan For Every Part (PFEP). Doing a PFEP requires heavy data analysis and physical changes to inventory locations, bin sizes, and logistics programs. It requires a detailed look at every part and it leads to healthy dialogue with suppliers about how to get things aligned. By the way, suppliers are usually happy to engage in the process because they are tired of the expedites and schedule changes. My recommendation is to attack this issue in small chunks. Prioritize the parts or suppliers that are causing the most pain. Get the value stream aligned on those, then rinse and repeat.

Ineffective supply base management

Supply base management is the practice of deciding on the suppliers with whom you will do business and the nature of the relationship. Supply base management answers questions like:

- Will this product be single-sourced or dual-sourced?

- Will it be produced domestically or in a low-cost country?

- Will the relationship be strategic or transactional?

- Will there be a long-term commitment or will items be purchased on a spot-buy basis?

Issues can arise when the needs of the supply base differ from the way it is structured. Let's look at a couple examples:

Example 1:

There is a part that is designed for a given product that can only be produced by Supplier X because they hold a patent on it. However, the purchasing group has been very heavy-handed with the supplier, demanding price reductions and payment term extensions. This has created an adversarial relationship with the supplier and, as a result, the supplier has made the company a low priority. This translates to poor responsiveness and missed deliveries, but since this is a patented product, the company has no options. In this case, the supplier is being treated as a commodity supplier when they should be treated like a strategic partner.

Example 2:

Part X is commonly used and can be sourced from multiple suppliers, both domestic and foreign. In order to achieve the lowest possible price, spending was consolidated and awarded to a Chinese supplier. The relationship was working fine until a longshoreman's strike on the West Coast led to stock-outs. Purchasing scrambled to re-engage with other suppliers only to find that they sold their capacity to other customers. In this case, a sole-source strategy was employed when a dual-source strategy may have been prudent to mitigate risk.

There is an art to establishing the right relationships with suppliers and the right answer isn't always obvious. I was the CEO of Intek Plastics when Hurricane Katrina hit the Gulf of Mexico. My company was in Minnesota, so those problems felt very distant. About three weeks after the hurricane hit, we received a force majeure letter from our sole-source plastic supplier stating that we were on allocation and would not be receiving all of the product that we had requested. The supply of natural gas, a key ingredient in the manufacture of plastic resin, had been disrupted by the hurricane and stocks were going to run out. Intuition might suggest that we would have been better off dual-sourced so we had a backup supplier. However, in this case, every plastic supplier had been disrupted. Our supplier worked with us in a very positive way to navigate the disruption, which was due largely to our continued commitment and loyalty to them. Sole-sourcing turned out to be the right approach to mitigate risk in this situation.

Supply bases should not be tampered with lightly. You will likely need to live with the consequences for years. However, if there are areas where the supply base strategy is creating operational performance issues, they need to be addressed in order to create a high-performance supply chain and factory.

I recommend using a simple four-square to determine the appropriate strategy for each supplier and compare it to the current strategy. The four-square is shown below:

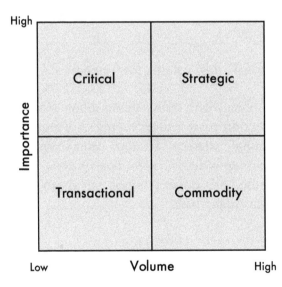

The x-axis is volume. This is the volume of business that you do with the supplier, relative to other suppliers. The y-axis is importance. This answers the question, "How screwed are we if they went out of business tomorrow?" If your office paper supplier went under tomorrow, you'd be back in business with one phone call. However, if the supplier of a patented product went out of business, you might be in a world of hurt that could impact production for months.

Commodity – high volume/low importance

> The strategy with commodity suppliers is to strive for the lowest prices. These products typically have an open marketplace and pricing is often transparent. Tactics include frequent bidding, consolidation of supply to get volume discounts, and striving for numerous concessions on non-price items such as payment terms, inventory, and logistics.

Transactional – low volume/low importance

> The strategy with transactional suppliers is to achieve low transaction costs. Office supplies are a great example of this supply strategy. We don't want to spend $75 to cut a purchase order for a $3 box of pens. Having online ordering and seamless billing are appropriate strategies for this supply base.

Critical – low volume/high importance

> Critical suppliers are a danger zone and the strategy is to get them out of the critical quadrant. An example of a

critical item might be a specialized motor that is needed for an important piece of equipment to run, and the lead time for a replacement motor is six months. In order to get this item out of the critical quadrant, you might switch to an off-the-shelf motor or hold a replacement motor in stock at the local distributor.

Strategic – high volume/high importance

Strategic suppliers are just what the name implies—strategic. They provide something that isn't easily replaced and they do considerable volume with you. The approach with strategic suppliers is to establish a partnering-style relationship. These relationships are often characterized as win-win and they operate with transparency for mutual gain.

These relationships take time, energy, and executive-level support, which means companies can only sustain a few strategic suppliers.

If suppliers are not performing and they don't seem responsive, there may be a smoking gun in the nature of the supply base relationship. These can take time to repair, but it's necessary to get to the root of the problem or the issues are likely to persist.

Weak sales and operations planning

Sales and operations planning (SOP) creates a forward-looking plan, usually three to twelve months into the future that aligns the sales forecast with operational capabilities. When a robust SOP is in place, fluctuations in demand are predicted in advance and the operations team—including the supply chain—can adjust.

I'll be addressing sales and operations planning later in this chapter, so I won't explore it further here. Suffice it to say, if the supply chain is not given adequate time to adjust to a new expectation, such as an increase in demand for a product line, you can expect that the supplier will struggle until they can address their capacity constraints, which are typically people and equipment.

Sometimes when we're in the heat of battle within our facilities, we forget about suppliers, and we think that somehow they are sitting on an unlimited capacity to meet our needs. That is no truer than the belief that our factory is sitting on an unlimited supply of capacity to meet our customers' needs. If we don't integrate the supply chain into a robust SOP process, we can expect that supplier capacity will be out of step with our needs.

If a weak SOP has resulted in the factory getting behind, then taking action to get caught up is the first order of business. Once the factory is caught up, improving the SOP process will help to avoid the same predicament in the future.

Core #7: Inventory

Accountants tell us that inventory is an asset, and Lean tells us that inventory is a waste. Regardless of the label we apply, inventory is an absolute necessity in every supply chain that I've seen. We can strive towards one-piece flow that eliminates inventory, but for now, inventory is a practical necessity. It creates a buffer to cover everyday situations such as:

- Long supplier lead times

- Long setup times

- Inconsistent quality

- Mismatched cycle times

- Batch operations (e.g., nesting of parts on a sheet of steel to optimize yield)

- Transportation costs (delivering a truckload at a time)

- Erratic customer demand

There are several tools and techniques for managing inventory. There are replenishment systems based on actual consumption, like Kanban, and there are others that use forecasts to predict consumption to determine when to replenish inventories. Regardless of the mechanisms for triggering the building or buying of more stock, the inventory needs to be in control.

My second job out of college was in information technology. I was a programmer and then a project leader, implementing custom-developed software at a large OEM. One of the projects that I led was the implementation of a finished goods warehouse inventory and logistics system. The first attempt to implement the software failed because we were trying to automate the complexities of the business. There were pockets of inventory throughout the plant and there was no clear accountability for it—among other things.

Following the failed implementation, we regrouped to figure out a game plan. The company needed a better system, but we had to do some things differently. I got a few of the operations and IT people together and we locked ourselves in a room to set out our guiding principles for inventory control. Here is what we came up with:

1. There must be physical control of the inventory. That means a designated place for everything. The warehouse needs to be organized and labeled clearly. There must be space to accommodate unexpected overflow.

2. Whenever feasible, inventory space should be contiguous. It should be clear where the entry and exit points are to the warehouse space.

3. There must be clear accountability for transactions, with limited people putting and pulling inventory from the locations.

4. There needs to be a clear accountability structure in place for inventory control and accuracy. The person responsible for inventory control should also be responsible for the people transacting inventory on the floor.

5. Planning processes need to be in place to manage inventories and adjust levels as business conditions warrant.

6. Processes for checking on inventory accuracy and adherence to inventory management must be established and followed.

Once we implemented these six principles and simplified the business, the software implementation went smoothly. Today, these are still solid ground rules for establishing inventory control. It seems that these days we get wrapped up with inventory planning techniques and lose sight of the basics about space, organization, and roles and responsibilities.

Inventory control is a great litmus test for leadership discipline. It's easy to let slip because it's not visible and in your face, but solid inventory control practices are critical to a healthy organization. If a team can demonstrate strong inventory control discipline, they are likely able to implement and sustain other Core 10 practices as well.

Core #8: Sales and Operations Planning

Sales and operations planning (SOP) is the practice of preparing a mid-range plan—typically three to twelve months—that integrates the sales forecast and production plan. It creates a common view that is agreed upon by the executive team. When done well, it creates harmony between sales, operations, finance, and HR. Everyone is working from the same playbook and the same assumptions.

The lack of a robust SOP process is one of the most common issues that I see. Organizations get surprised by a change in order volume and operations are thrown into a reactive mode trying to adjust. One of the realities that manufacturers must face is that production capacity is relatively static and it takes time to change—both up and down. With the tight labor market, headcount additions come in small increments and with significant investments in recruiting, onboarding, and training. Likewise, if order volume dips, companies are hesitant to lay off their workforce—the workforce that they've worked so hard to acquire and train.

One client recently paid the price for a weak SOP. After a slow 2017, orders skyrocketed in 2018. This is a great problem to have, but it caught them flat-footed. The company had a weak

SOP process, and they relied on their annual budgeting process to set expectations for volume and staffing. As a result, they didn't anticipate the tidal wave of orders. Plant management was understandably hesitant to add people given the weakness from 2017. In their mind, their job was to hit the budget. However, orders kept coming and the backlog started to climb. The plant tried to adjust by working overtime, but it wasn't enough. Lead times were four times longer than historical norms. On-time delivery plummeted. Not only did the plant react too late, but the entire supply chain was also behind the curve. When the plant finally decided to increase throughput, the supply chain wasn't prepared, so throughput remained stuck. The plant wasn't positioned to serve customers well and, as a result, customers started turning to their competition. The company, which had a great reputation for customer service, got a very serious black eye.

The sales team blamed operations for not keeping up with demand and operations blamed sales for not providing a decent forecast. Both sides were right. Everyone was trying to do the right thing, but the lack of integration created a mismatch between customer requirements and the capacity in the factory.

Some people get hung up on the technical aspects of an SOP process, like elaborate forecasting algorithms. However, I think that the energy aimed at sophistication is misguided. The deep benefit of an SOP process is its power to align the senior leadership team. The SOP process forces the team to turn toward the future and make educated guesses about capabilities that will be needed.

Determining the future capacity of operations is critical. If you guess too high, you'll have a bloated cost structure. If you guess too low, you won't have the capacity needed to take care of customers. Determining the future capacity of the plant is going to be one of the biggest determinants of profitability and it needs to be a team decision, not just an operations decision.

The SOP process consists of four milestones that occur each month at regular intervals:

1. The sales forecast is updated to roll forward one more month. Ideally, the forecast has product-line level detail. This happens early in the month.

2. Within 10 days of the sales forecast having been issued, the operations team develops a plan to respond to the forecast. This plan includes headcount changes, inventory needs, and capital investment.

3. After operations has their plan together, mid-level management reviews the sales and operations plans to reconcile points of contention. They then prepare a recommendation for senior management.

4. The last step is for the senior management team to review and approve the recommendation from mid-management. This should not be a rubber stamp. There should be considerable discussion and debate.

SOP is a fundamental process for managing a manufacturing operation. A sound, simple SOP process enables the right business discussions and promotes executive team health. Nobody can guess the future precisely, but a monthly look into the crystal ball gets everyone aligned and marching to the beat of the same drummer.

Core #9: Data and Measurement

I have a confession to make. I have vacillated on the importance of data. Early in my career, I was a programmer and a big advocate of plentiful and accurate data. Later, as I became familiar with Lean concepts, I shied away from data because I felt that visual management could supplant the need for information systems and the mountains of data needed to make them run. At this point, I've come full circle. I believe that having a core set of accurate data is necessary for the operation of a stable and healthy factory.

Einstein said, "Make things as simple as possible, but no simpler." I think this is the right mantra for data in a manufacturing company. I have been in factories that live on both ends of the spectrum. I've seen plants that have almost no data and they feel like they're flying blind. I've also seen plants that are buried in data to the point that they don't know what to do with all of it.

The goal is to find the middle ground where you have the data that is needed to run the business without incurring unnecessary expenses and effort. I'll walk you through the process by looking at three categories of data:

1. Process data

2. Financial data

3. Transactional data

Process data

Process data tells us if a process is working as intended. Examples of process data would include:

- On-time delivery

- Productivity

- First-pass yield

- Percent of calls that roll to voicemail

- Machine uptime

- Days to close the books

While it's possible to measure hundreds of processes, I recommend that each level of the organization has seven to ten process metrics that they watch. Choosing the right measure is often an art. Focusing on seven to ten measures forces leadership teams to develop a deep understanding of the processes that truly move the needle.

The senior leadership team struggles with this the most. There is a tendency to want to measure processes that are the responsibility of a functional group at a lower level in the company. For example, the senior leadership team may feel the need to measure safety incidences or productivity. While these are important, they are the responsibility of the operations function. Rather than tracking these, I recommend that the senior leadership team focuses on process measures that are tied to strategy.

Example 1: Let's say that a company has a strategy to grow revenue in a new market. In order to do so, they have chosen to compete with best-in-industry lead times. They're going to accommodate for these short lead times by holding inventory of the product family for a new market. In this case, the senior leadership may choose to watch metrics related to this inventory. Perhaps the fulfillment rate or inventory accuracy of this product line would give the best insight into the execution of the strategy. Note that the measure is focused on the specific product line tied to the strategy. The operations team might look at plant-wide fulfillment rates, but the senior leadership team should be focused on strategic products.

Example 2: The company has decided that staffing is a strategic issue. In order to address the staffing challenges, they have decided to compete by making the work environment fun and engaging. In order to keep tabs on the pulse of the workforce, they might install a simple happiness indicator at the exit door (www.celpax. com). As workers leave, they simply press the red or green button depending on whether or not they had a good day. The device links to software that reports day-to-day and week-to-week results. This would give direct feedback about the effectiveness of creating a more fun and engaging work environment.

The senior leadership team is responsible for the establishment and execution of strategy; their data and measures should reflect the importance of understanding strategic processes. That said, the senior leadership team must do the heavy lifting to ensure that nonstrategic but important measures are being tracked within the functions. I'll address this further in the next section on the operating system.

Financial data

Good process data will provide strong indicators of financial performance, but it must be validated periodically with official financial reports. Financial reports answer the question, "We thought X was going to happen. Is that what really happened?"

I am continually surprised at the relative weakness of financial reporting in many companies. Typical issues include:

- Slow turnaround time closing the books each month, making the data very outdated.

- Erratic results driven by accounting adjustments such as inventory adjustments or accruals for bonuses or rebates.

- Lack of insight about real spending trends due to the nature of standard cost accounting and absorption.

Back in the 1950s, W. Edwards Deming introduced the Plan-Do-Check-Adjust cycle as a model for implementing continuous improvement. The essence of the model is to plan improvements (Plan), implement them (Do), see if the changes had the desired impact (Check), and make appropriate course corrections (Adjust). Financial statements provide the necessary "Check" in the Plan-Do-Check-Adjust cycle. Weak or obtuse financial reporting leaves an executive team flying blind.

In the mid-2000s, I took over the role of the VP of Operations at a contract manufacturer that was struggling financially. I sat through the normal, monthly financial review, and I became increasingly frustrated and alarmed. I heard about absorption variances and material variances, and I saw a hundred numbers flash before my eyes. I finally stopped the CFO and asked, "Are we okay or aren't we? Where do I need to drive improvements? I can't decipher what you're showing me." This prompted a 10-minute nonsensical regurgitation of what the system was telling him. I knew that this accounting system was compliant with Generally Accepted Accounting Principles (GAAP), but it was pretty much worthless to me as a leader trying to figure out what areas I needed to attack.

One of the first changes that I like to see in the accounting system is a move from a standard cost P&L to a direct cost P&L. A standard cost P&L is usually formatted like this:

Revenue	$100
COGS	$60
Purchase Price Variance	$3
Absorption Variance	$8
Production Variance	$6
Gross Margin	$23
Expenses	
Sales & Marketing	$15
IT	$1
R&D	$3
Admin	$2
Profit	$2

In this P&L, manufacturing costs are reported relative to a standard cost for products. The issue is that this comparison obfuscates the actual numbers. This inevitably leads to questions like, "Did the standards change?" and "Are the standards accurate?" (They are almost always out of date and inaccurate.) What's more, there is a line that reads "Absorption Variance." That's an accounting mechanism that tries to adjust overhead allocations based on the standard amount of volume that is expected to be produced. It is an algorithmic method for the accountants to produce a GAAP-compliant P&L, but it has almost no bearing on the performance of the factory and provides little insight.

When leadership teams are faced with a standard cost P&L, they usually nod politely as if they are getting some insight from it, but deep down they aren't. Worse still, they may take the wrong actions. For example, to reduce Absorption Variance, the plant needs to produce more, which means that they may hire more people and build inventory. This would be the absolute wrong thing to do if the underlying issue is that orders are soft. The plant would have added cost and built inventory at a time that they should be moving in the other direction.

I prefer a P&L that shows actual costs. Shown below is an example of direct cost P&L:

Revenue	$100
Materials	$60
Value-add Revenue	$40
Costs:	
Labor	$8
Scrap	$1
Other production costs	$7
Gross Margin	$24
Inventory Adjustment	$1
Net Gross Margin	$23
Expenses	
Sales & Marketing	$15
IT	$1
R&D	$3
Admin	$2
Profit	$2

There are several reasons why I prefer this layout:

- Materials are subtracted to get to value-added revenue. This provides a clearer picture of the revenues that a company is collecting from customers to cover costs. I have seen contract manufacturers that thought they were growing but were merely passing along material cost increases.

- Actual costs are shown rather than standards and variances. When these are plotted month by month, it is clear when there are cost changes.

- Inventory adjustments are isolated so that the leadership team can see the impact of changes on the income statement. Generally, I don't think that senior leaders should feel positive about an improvement in profitability if it was driven by an increase in inventory. Likewise, they should not feel negatively if profitability eroded due to a decrease in inventory.

This type of income statement is easy to implement and it can be done in parallel with the traditional financial statements. It's worth noting the revenue, gross margin, and profit do not change. This approach is not about making the numbers look better. Instead, it is aimed at providing better insight into the data.

Transactional data

Transactional data, as the name suggests, is needed to support day-to-day transactions—including sales, customer service, engineering, scheduling, shipping, and invoicing.

When I visit factories, the management team often says, "We're different. We don't crank out a thousand of the same thing every day. We have very high variety." It seems that everyone thinks that they are the only ones dealing with complexity. We need to dispel this myth. Low-variety, high-volume manufacturing migrated to low-cost countries in the late 20th century, and U.S. manufacturing is predominantly lower-volume, higher-variety manufacturing. Customers want what they want and that has led to product proliferation, high-variety, lower-volume production runs and increased complexity.

Information systems are necessary to support the complexity of modern factories, and yet many companies have let their data fall into terrible disrepair. I hear statements like:

- Our customer due dates aren't realistic.

- Our prints don't reflect how the product is really made.

- We don't include the time for QC and outside services in our routing, so the schedules are all messed up.

- The actual production times don't reflect the current processes.

Strong companies recognize that accurate transactional data is an asset to be maintained, just like the physical assets of buildings and equipment. Once data has deteriorated, it can require substantial effort to correct it, so it is better to have the governance processes in place to ensure that data is maintained accurately.

Data and measurement: Wrap-up

We've reviewed three categories of data: process data, financial data, and transactional data. When working properly, these provide insight and knowledge to enable the efficient operation of a factory. However, when the data isn't accurate or is being presented improperly, it can be unhelpful or misleading.

Fixing data is not nearly as sexy as making changes on the shop floor, but it can be one of the most important core systems. When it functions well, it is an enabler of effective management.

Core #10: The Operating System

The term "operating system" is a bit nebulous. Some people describe it as the way they run their business, although I don't find that terribly helpful. I'll take a shot at making it a bit more concrete. I define an operating system as a set of practices and principles that are used to define and implement the company's strategy and objectives. It isn't the strategy itself—it's how the strategy gets converted to reality.

When the operating system is working well, people are focused and aligned, and things are getting done. When the operating system is not working well, activities are not aligned and there are disputes about the priorities. There are eight ingredients in a strong operating system:

1. Core Values

   Mentioning core values often elicits eye rolls because many organizations treat them as little more than conference room wallpaper. That's not what I'm talking about. I'm talking about the deeply held values of the organization. These values define who will fit in the company and who will not. Core values describe the behaviors you reward and the behaviors that will not be tolerated. If people do not fit the core values, they must be removed from the company because they are eroding the culture every day. This holds true even if a person is excellent in their role.

When I help leadership teams define their core values, we begin by asking each person to think of a person that they deeply admire. We then have them write down all the words that describe what they admire about them. We put those words on the board and start filtering them until we get to four. These are four that need to stick in their gut. The team needs to be nodding their heads, saying "That's us!"

One of my clients recently came up with these four core values:

- Grit

- Accountability

- Caring and Supportive

- Team Success

They went on to add a story to each of these to describe what they meant. Then they shared them with everyone in their company. It provided a language for them to talk with their employees about the behaviors that are important to them and it had a positive impact on performance and engagement.

Core values are a key ingredient for creating a healthy, aligned team. They promote unity, leading to high performance and a willingness to work together.

2. Value Proposition

The value proposition states clearly and succinctly who your customers are and how you choose to compete to win their business. One company may choose to compete on price while another one wants to offer the most sophisticated products in the marketplace. Another company may highlight their responsiveness when another might emphasize their ability to integrate with customers.

The key is that there must be a direction. Companies that fail to choose or choose differently depending on the customer that is in front of them today will send their teams on a winding path to nowhere.

Let's contrast two companies with different value propositions. Company A has chosen to compete by providing very short lead times and excellent customer service. They hold significant inventories so that customers never run out and they've installed distribution centers right next to their customers. They also staff their customer service center to match the production schedule of their customers, so that there is always a live person to address any issues. They charge a premium price for this high level of service and they seek out customers who value what they offer. This is clearly a high-service and high-cost value proposition.

Company B sells products similar to company A, but they choose to compete by being the lowest-price provider. In order to provide low prices and still make a profit, expenses are cut to the bone. Manufacturing is done in low-cost countries and they require full-container orders from the customer. They have a small customer service staff and the phone is answered by an automated message. Lead times often extend to six or more weeks due to transportation times.

There is nothing inherently good or bad about either of these value propositions, but they are not compatible together. Companies that are clear on their value proposition will be able to execute that strategy clearly, whereas companies that vacillate on their value proposition will end up with a mishmash of capabilities that leaves employees and customers confused.

3. Organization Structure

Organizations need to know who is responsible for what and a strong operating system provides this clarity. The traditional organization structure shows a hierarchy, with each box on the hierarchy representing a different function (e.g., sales, marketing, manufacturing, purchasing, IT, and accounting). This kind of structure clarifies who is responsible for these functions, but organizations tend to need more insight.

A common challenge is that processes flow across functional boundaries. They don't live within them. For example, a customer order starts in the sales function, then it moves into the order entry function, followed by the scheduling function, manufacturing, distribution, and after-sale support. Each of these functions is managed by a different person, so who owns the customer fulfillment process?

The same can be said for many processes. Who owns inventory? It is affected by planning, purchasing, manufacturing, receiving, and inventory control.

Some companies are addressing this by going to matrix organizations where a person is assigned ownership of a process while other people own the function. For example, one person can be named as the person in charge of inventory, even though this includes multiple functions. This structure can be very effective in organizations that are healthy, aligned, and have little issue with internal politics. However, it can muddy the waters and create confusion in organizations that have low trust and low team health.

Another common issue is centralized or shared service functions. Let's take purchasing. Often, the function of selecting suppliers and negotiating arrangements is done by a centralized purchasing group. This group may be very far removed from the day-to-day problems arising from a supplier, such as poor quality or late deliveries. When these problems occur, it needs to be clear who has responsibility for resolving the issue. Is it the plant, purchasing, or both?

There is no perfect organization structure, and companies sway back and forth as the warts of one structure become visible. The pendulum swings to another structure, and eventually those warts also show, so it swings back. In many cases, this continual shifting of the structure results from two things: 1) There is poor leadership team health, which is inhibiting the communication and cooperation needed to make any structure work, and 2) the work has not been done to clarify the roles and responsibilities clearly, particularly around the edges, where one group needs to interface with another group.

4. Strategy Implementation

Implementing the company strategy is an essential function of the leadership team, but most organizations struggle to make the strategic plan a reality.

While there are a number of published approaches to assist with the implementation of strategies, they have several things in common:

- Simplify the strategic plan to one or two pages.

- Focus short-term activities on one or two vital initiatives.

- Establish a weekly meeting pattern to check on the status and make course corrections.

- Confront the reality of the day-to-day workload of people.

If the operating system is strong, everyone in the company should have clarity about the strategy, the short-term priorities, and their role in making it a reality. This enables the company to continue to achieve strong results today while still building for the future.

5. Systems and Processes

Good systems and processes can make average people excel and poor processes can make great people look terrible. Having well-defined simple processes that are understood and followed by everyone enables consistent, repeatable, and scalable execution.

Systems and processes are related but different. A process is a set of procedures, information, and actions to accomplish a specific task. A system is a collection of processes aimed at achieving a broader business objective. For example, the quality management system is comprised of processes that ensure gauges are calibrated, supplier quality is tracked, inspections are occurring, etc. These processes make up the quality management system, which has a business goal of ensuring that customer expectations are met.

The operating system should identify the core systems and processes of the business. In this book I've recommended 10 core systems, but this list should be tailored to your business needs. It may be desirable to add systems for sales, marketing, and administration to the list.

Once the core systems are identified, the key processes involved in building those systems should be identified.

Take care not to go overboard by creating an abundance of process documents with a hyper-specific level of detail. This can turn into busywork that yields minimal benefit. Every company has people who are extremely detail-oriented, and for them there is no detail not worth overanalyzing. I recommend limiting the operating system to 10 to 15 core systems that deeply impact the performance of the company. Each of those core systems should have no more than five building-block processes.

The processes need to be documented, but documentation is just the beginning. Processes only work when everyone is following them. Having good, repeatable processes is an action, not a document. Taiichi Ohno, one of the founders of the Toyota Production System, called it standard work. He said that standard work is the best way, followed by everybody until a new best way is found. He also said that without standard work there can be no improvement.

Getting people to follow standard work can be a tremendous challenge, especially in organizations that have a long history of letting people do their own thing. In some cases, it is the history of just-get-it-done cowboys who got the company to where it is today. These people will resist the need for consistent execution of a standard process.

Implementing robust processes that are followed by everyone will test the change management muscles of the company. Later in this book we'll discuss the leadership needed to create sustained change.

6. Meetings

I know, I know. Meetings are awful. It's a reputation that has been painfully earned. I don't blame anyone for being skeptical about the necessity of meetings as part of an operating system, but hear me out.

Meetings aren't bad. Bad meetings are bad. Unfortunately, most of the meetings that we attend are awful. However, when done well, meetings offer great benefits:

- Person-to-person connections are created, improving team health.

- Alignment is created because all people hear the same message at once, removing points of confusion.

- It is more efficient than a series of one-on-one meetings.

- Everyone's voice gets heard by the others, leading to better, team-based solutions and team commitment.

The operating system should define two meeting parameters. First, it should define the number of regularly occurring meetings that are integral to running the business. I'll call this the meeting regimen. Second, the operating system should clarify the tone, tenor, and expectations of meetings so that they are effective. Let's look at each of these.

Regularly Occurring Meetings: The Meeting Regimen

Regularly occurring meetings enable the organization to address normal business situations as a matter of routine. A strong meeting structure gives the right information to the right people so that they can make the right decision in a timely manner.

Examples of regularly occurring meetings:

What	When	Who
Strategic planning	2 days, annual, 4th Quarter	Executive team
Quarterly review	1 day, quarterly	Executive team and each function
Staff meeting	1 hour, weekly	All managers and their team
Stand-up/Tier meetings	15 minutes, daily	Production supervisors and their team
Board meetings	1 day, quarterly	Executive team and board of directors
Strategy implementation reviews	30 minutes, weekly	Strategy implementation team
Quality system review	2 hours, quarterly	Executive team, next-level managers
Safety system review	1 hour, quarterly	Operations leadership, CEO

What	When	Who
Sales forecast review (part of sales and operations planning)	1 hour, monthly	Sales leadership, ops leadership, master planner
Operations plan review (part of sales and operations planning)	1 hour, monthly	Ops leadership, master planner, accounting leadership
SOP review	1 hour, monthly	Executive team

These are just examples and aren't meant to be prescriptive. However, they should give you a sense for the kind of meetings that you could introduce into your operating system. Ensuring this meeting pulse is present in the operating system signals to the organization that these meetings are important. They are where the business is run and should not be missed.

It's common for the meeting regimen to change over time as the needs of the business change. For instance, if staffing the shop floor is a key success factor, you may want to add a regular meeting pulse to discuss the talent system. In fact, there may be a weekly meeting to review progress against filling open slots followed by a quarterly meeting to review the overall talent management system.

Once the meeting regimen has been established, we need to turn our attention to making the meetings effective.

Effective Meetings:

As you can see from the list above, it's quite possible that there will be a number of meetings in the meeting regimen. Meetings must add value and contribute to the performance of the business. They cannot become mere overhead and bureaucracy. One of my litmus tests for the effectiveness of meetings is to assess whether people would raise a ruckus if the meeting were discontinued.

There are five rules that ensure meetings are effective and value adding:

1. Meetings must have a clearly stated purpose that describes the actions or decisions that should come from the meeting. Sharing information is not a valid purpose. Here are a few examples of purpose statements:

Meeting	Purpose
Tier 1 shop floor meeting	Identify performance gaps, determine countermeasures, and assign responsibility
Quarterly quality review	Recommend top three priorities for improvement for the next 90 days
Weekly staff meeting	Identify top issues and take corrective actions

2. Meetings must start on time and end on time. Period. Meetings that start late or run long are disrespectful of people's time; they indicate a lack of discipline.

Early in my career, I had the benefit of a great mentor, Jim Cutler, who was an executive at Danaher during the early days of Lean in the U.S. Jim was at my company facilitating a kaizen event and at one point he joined me during my weekly staff meeting. After the meeting ended, he made a simple comment: "Rob, the meeting started five minutes late." I responded, "Yes, that's pretty normal around here." He said, "You expect the shop floor to produce to a precise schedule. How do you expect to make that happen if you can't even start a meeting on time?" Ouch. That was one of those moments of candor that hurt at the time, but it had a lasting impact that helped shape my view of the power of details and execution.

3. Meetings must have full attendance. If a meeting is in the operating system, it's important that the full complement of participants are there. Vacations and death are acceptable excuses for not attending, but that's about it.

At one company, the VP of sales had a habit of not attending the weekly senior leadership staff meeting because there was often a client visit or a quote that he deemed a much higher priority. It was frustrating for the other members of the executive team because there were topics that needed the voice of the sales team and that voice was absent. After numerous discussions with him, we finally got to the heart of the matter. His passion was sales and he didn't want to be part of the leadership team. He just wanted to sell. We accommodated his request by making him an individual contributor. Another person was named to the executive team in his stead.

4. There must be a defined agenda. While the specifics of each meeting will be unique, there is a common flow:

    - A check-in on the status of prior commitments. This provides accountability to the team.

    - A quick review of key metrics related to the meeting purpose. This provides data that can give insight into the current state of affairs.

    - A time to discuss issues and determine corrective actions. This section, which should comprise the majority of the meeting, keeps things action oriented. Good facilitation is required to ensure the dialogue remains focused.

    - A wrap-up that clarifies actions and owners. The meeting is then self-scored on a scale of 1 to 10, which enables continuous improvement. Lower scores should be discussed to understand what could be improved.

5. Minutes must be captured and distributed. The minutes should reflect attendees, the issues discussed, and the actions that are taken.

Prioritize the Core 10: Wrap-up

In this section, I've outlined 10 core systems that are essential to every manufacturer. When your factory is struggling, step back and assess the health of these 10 systems. You'll want to view the factory as if you were an outsider. Perhaps you can pretend to be a board member or maybe a potential acquirer. Look at the big picture and pose the question about the underlying health of each of these core systems. You will find that in almost all cases, struggles in a factory can be traced back to weakness in one of the core systems. Use this insight as a guide and a compass to focus your improvement efforts.

EXECUTE WITH DISCIPLINE

Execute with Discipline: Introduction

Now we come to the final and perhaps the most difficult stage of the Fix-A-Factory journey—implementing changes. If you've been following this process sequentially, the leadership team has set the stage so that the organization is ready to accept change. You've done the digging to reveal the issues, and you've assessed where you stand against the Core 10 processes. All of that is for naught if we don't translate it into action to make things happen. In this section, we'll cover some of the principles and tools that will enable your organization to execute with discipline.

Execute with Discipline: 90-Day Cadence

What does 90-day cadence mean? In a nutshell, it is the practice of setting priorities for the next 90 days, working hard on those priorities, and then reprioritizing for the next 90 days.

Why 90 days?

There is something magical about 90 days. It is a time frame that is long enough to allow an organization to accomplish big things, yet it is short enough that it creates some urgency. Many companies set annual goals and priorities, but at the end of the year they have often fallen far short of achieving them. One of the reasons for the low success rate is that a year seems like a long time. If you have an entire year to implement a project, it's easy to set it aside and procrastinate while you put your attention on the urgent issues of the day.

However, if you have 90 days to complete a project, the timing starts to feel very real. Let's take a simple example of a project to hire a steel buyer. On the surface, it seems completely reasonable to hire a new buyer within 90 days, but consider these milestones:

- Complete job description

- Get approval from senior leaders to hire

- Post ad on job site board

- Gather all applicants

- Filter to a list of top five

- Conduct interviews

- Conduct second round of interviews for top two candidates

- Prepare offer

- Candidate acceptance and two-week notice

- Pre-employment checks

- First day—begin onboarding

When you start putting dates to those milestones, you can see that there's a lot to get done. You get a small pit in your stomach as you think, "Holy cow, I better get started." A 90-day cadence forces the translation from a conceptual goal into concrete, specific actions.

Another benefit of a 90-day cadence is that it allows a leadership team to course correct and reprioritize every 90 days. Business conditions change. Any of the following might warrant a new set of priorities:

- Winning a client who needs a new capability.

- A quality issue that has emerged in the field.

- A project that was unsuccessful in the last 90 days due to some other factor that must be addressed.

- A new product launch has been delayed.

- An initiative is not generating the expected results, and corrective action is required.

This list could go on and on. The point is that things change, and you don't want to be locked into the priorities from the beginning of the year if those priorities have become obsolete.

The last benefit of the 90-day cadence is that it gets the leadership team realigned. One of the comments that I hear from companies that have embraced a 90-day cadence is, "I really didn't want to take a day off-site to set our priorities, but I'm so glad we did. We were starting to get fragmented, and now we're back on the same page." The 90-day cadence forces the leadership team to lift their heads up every 90 days, look around, and reset so that they can put their heads back down and go execute.

The 90-day cadence is a form of the Plan-Do-Check-Adjust cycle, and it's a critical enabler of disciplined execution.

Prioritize and focus: the quarterly reset

The 90-day cadence requires that a leadership team establishes priorities for the upcoming 90 days. This usually involves a full-day meeting once a quarter where the team hashes out the competing interests and lands on the vital few priorities. I call this the Quarterly Reset.

The quarterly reset day consists of the following:

- **A review of the prior quarter**
  The team takes an hour to look back at the last quarter to see how they did against their scorecard, business results, and priorities. The key lessons learned are captured.

- **A review of the company's longer-term objectives**
  Before diving into the process of deciding priorities for the next 90 days, it is helpful to step back and review the company's strategies and objectives. This would include a review of the one-year goals and objectives and the

three-to-five-year longer-term goals. This review helps to establish context as you enter the prioritization process.

- **Identification of all possible projects**
  This is a brainstorming session to get every possible thing that could be a priority on the table. This is a mind-clearing, mental health exercise. Put them all on the whiteboard. Having 70 to 100 ideas is common.

- **Filter to the vital few**
  Through active debate, discussion, voting, and other facilitation techniques, the list is whittled down to a vital few. I like to limit the list to five initiatives. Getting a long list down to five forces the leadership team to do the hard work and heavy lifting to say "no" while putting energy towards a few well-placed bets.

- **Write the charters**
  I'm a big fan of one-page project charters. A charter defines the scope, objectives, team members, and milestones of a project. Writing the charters, reviewing them, and editing them can consume two to three hours of the meeting, and it's worth every minute.

The benefit of writing the charter is increased alignment of the leadership team. It is common for the first draft of the charter to describe a project that is very different than what the rest of the leadership team had in mind. The charter can help avoid weeks of misalignment and confusion as the project leader heads one direction and the rest of the leadership team is headed in another direction.

Project charters also dramatically improve the odds of successful implementation. Projects often stall because the project leader doesn't have clarity about what to do next. Writing the project charter, including the milestones, forces the project leader to critically think about the roadmap for implementing the project.

Do yourself a favor and write the charters while you're together as a group. This single step will enable much more disciplined and rapid execution.

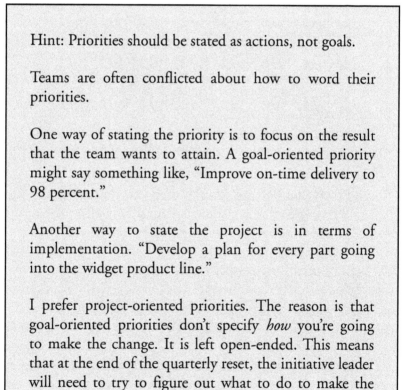

Hint: Priorities should be stated as actions, not goals.

Teams are often conflicted about how to word their priorities.

One way of stating the priority is to focus on the result that the team wants to attain. A goal-oriented priority might say something like, "Improve on-time delivery to 98 percent."

Another way to state the project is in terms of implementation. "Develop a plan for every part going into the widget product line."

I prefer project-oriented priorities. The reason is that goal-oriented priorities don't specify *how* you're going to make the change. It is left open-ended. This means that at the end of the quarterly reset, the initiative leader will need to try to figure out what to do to make the improvement. This follow-through often doesn't happen, which means that the goal-oriented priority turns into little more than an aspiration or target. Stating a desire to achieve 98 percent on-time delivery may feel like good executive leadership, but it is lacking. It's kicking the can down the road. The leadership team needs to place a bet on the actions that will lead to 98 percent on-time delivery.

If the leadership team doesn't know the right actions, which may very well be the case, there should be a follow-up to the quarterly reset to immediately pull together the people who would have insight about the best actions to take.

Remember that the purpose of the quarterly reset is to determine the actions for the next quarter, not just the ambitions for the quarter.

Cascade and synchronize

After the senior leadership team has created the top priorities for the next 90 days, it's time to cascade these priorities into the next levels of the organization. In smaller companies, it may be as simple as pulling everyone together and letting them know the priorities. In larger organizations, each functional leader will need to take the priorities to their team so they can create the next level of priorities for their teams. This often requires the functional teams (e.g., manufacturing, sales, product development) to conduct their own quarterly reset meetings.

A functional team can decide on two types of priorities and projects. The first type of priority is the one that directly supports the top-level priorities of the company. The second type of priority is the one that's important within the functional group but is not necessarily tied to the company priorities.

The projects that directly support the top-level priorities need to get top billing. Once those projects are scoped and resourced, then second-level priorities can be added to the list.

Once the priorities of the second level have been developed, it's time for the senior leadership team to get back together and evaluate them holistically. The senior leadership team should look for red flags, such as:

- Groups that are overcommitted.

- Requests for resources that are beyond the means of the company.

- Projects that seem out of sequence.

- Lack of clarity and specificity in the project charters.

After the senior leadership has reconciled the initiatives, the main functional groups in the company should be aligned. From there, it's time to implement the changes.

Deselect and Deselect Some More

Every single organization that I've worked with takes on too much for the first quarter or two that they practice 90-day discipline. By nature, we tend to think that we can get more done than we really can, and we also tend to minimize the time commitment needed for the day-to-day management of the business.

You will not be able to dedicate 100 percent of your time to your priorities. In fact, I think you'll be lucky to dedicate 20 percent of your time to these priorities.

This means that the deselection of activities is vital. When I facilitate sessions with clients, a common refrain is, "But we *have* to do all of these." That is a trigger phrase for me. It's a sign of a leadership team that wants to avoid making the hard calls. Saying that all of these have to be done does not magically create the resources to make it realistic.

Focus and deselect. If you don't do it, your staff will do it for you and it will be unfocused, unaligned, and it won't lead to great results.

Weekly check-in

Now that you've launched a vital few initiatives for the next 90 days, we need to check in on the progress regularly to ensure that things are on track. Even top-priority projects can get derailed. Common issues include:

- An unforeseen resource constraint

- Poor project leadership

- A murky charter that has not created clarity about the project

- The discovery of a significant challenge

- Leaders continuing their pet projects

- A business crisis emerges, pulling people away from the project

These issues need to be flushed as early as possible. Remember, you have done the hard work to focus on a few mission-critical projects. The entire leadership team agreed that these are the highest priority initiatives to work on. You need to have a mindset that these projects will be completed or we'll die trying. 100 percent completion of every project may not happen, but 80 percent of the initiatives should get done.

The weekly check-in is the vehicle to see if the priorities are making progress. The check-in can be part of the weekly leadership staff meeting, but I recommend carving out time on the agenda specifically focused on reviewing the priorities—20 to 30 minutes should be enough.

I like to start by having each initiative leader simply say whether they are on target or off target against their milestones. Then the discussion can be opened up to get a brief status update and identification of emerging issues and challenges. If a project is losing momentum and has the potential to miss its objective, then corrective action must be taken.

The mindset of the leadership team should be reminiscent of the scene in *Apollo 13*, when Gene Kranz, the flight director, says, "We've never lost an American in space, we're sure as hell not gonna lose one on my watch! Failure is not an option." Perhaps that's a bit melodramatic, but the tone is right. Of the things that you could do, you chose a very small number that you felt would have the biggest impact on the company. These need to succeed! If the leadership team isn't feeling the urgency and drive to make these initiatives succeed, it's likely that you picked the wrong initiatives.

The weekly check-in is the Check and Adjust portion of the Plan-Do-Check-Adjust cycle. When projects are launched, all of the issues and challenges can't be anticipated. Checking the status weekly is the mechanism that allows the leadership team to make adjustments before it's too late. It also signals to the organization that these projects really are important. Your people pay attention to what you pay attention to. When they see you checking in and making the success of these projects a priority, they'll get aligned with the same priorities. Do the weekly check-ins. You won't regret it.

Execute with Discipline: Make it Stick

Starting change is easy. Staying with the program and making the changes permanent is a completely different animal. Fixing a factory requires more than a bandage or tourniquet. In this section, we'll cover some techniques for leading change that sticks.

How fast can we go?

We can only go as fast as the organization will let us go. Athletes understand this. Running fast out of the gate doesn't mean you'll get to the finish line first. If you aren't in good enough condition, you might have to slow your pace later in the race or, worse yet, you can injure yourself, hindering your ability to run at all. I don't know if it's part of the American culture or just part of being in the business world, but we like to go fast. However, like an athlete, it takes time and training to build the muscle, flexibility, and aerobic capacity to go fast all the way to the finish line.

We've probably all seen a bright, aggressive person loaded with great ideas for the company and they mash the gas pedal to implement their vision of the future. A few months later, the person is frustrated because he's finding that he's on an island and nobody is following him. When I was first exposed to Lean 20 years ago, I was one of these people. I was so excited by what I was learning. I wanted my plant to become Lean, and like an impetuous two-year-old, I wanted it *now*! I pushed hard and I learned firsthand what happens when an unstoppable force meets an immovable object. Sparks flew! As it turned out, I was not an unstoppable force and I became a movable object. I chose to leave the company. At the time, I blamed it on the organization's unwillingness to change, lack of vision, and lack of senior leadership. With time and maturity, I've come to accept that I was every bit as much to blame as anything because I didn't recognize the organization's readiness to change and I didn't adjust my approach to meet them where they were. I continue to run into people like the younger-me to this day.

There isn't a formula that will tell you exactly how fast you can go, but you can assess it subjectively. Some questions to ask include:

- How aligned and healthy is the leadership team?

- What has been the track record for sustaining previous changes?

- To what degree does the workforce trust leadership?

- Has there been a history of program-of-the-month?

- Is there a disciplined and rigorous change management method that addresses the structural and social implications of changes?

- Has change become a common experience and is it viewed positively? Are work teams asking for changes to be brought to their area?

- Has there been a recent history of changes leading to negative consequences, such as terminations or layoffs?

- Are the workers in the affected area resilient or are they delicate?

Answering these questions will give you an overall picture of the organization's ability to absorb change. It can also provide some direction about where you could focus to create a stronger base for faster implementation.

Even after reflecting and assessing your readiness for change, the only true way to test how fast you can go is to try. Using your operating system, you can establish the priorities for the next 90 days and take a shot at implementing them. At the end of 90 days, you'll have a much better feel for how much change the company can absorb. If you're like 99 percent of the people out there, you'll start by taking on too much; a number of changes won't get accomplished or they won't stick. When that happens, you know that you need to slow down a little and build up your capacity to hold change.

The key is to listen to the feedback you're getting. There are clear signs when the rate of change is exceeding the organization's ability to absorb the change. Here are some things to watch for:

- A lack of good results from the change.

- Criticism during townhall or all-employee meetings. This should not be written off as "resistance to change." The employees are telling you something.

- Increased spats, infighting, or political posturing. In other words, an erosion of team health.

- A lack of sustainment of changes. In this case, new changes look promising for a few weeks but then erode back to the old state.

- Confusion about the goals.

- Inability to get time or attention from key people.

- Missed deadlines on new initiatives.

- Increased turnover.

Consider these signals a blessing. They are the leading indicators suggesting that you could be headed towards difficult times if you stay the course and just plow ahead. When facing these warning signs, some will choose to be the against-all-odds cowboy that will persevere through all barriers. I suppose that this works occasionally, but it's painful and risky. These are the red-line tachometer gauge of your company. The more these signs appear, the closer you are to burning up your engine. It's time to let off the gas and maybe even press in the clutch before trying to move forward.

Going Fast: Lessons from Mario Kart

As I've mentioned earlier, I have a son who is on the autism spectrum and he's a big part of my life. We are fortunate that he is high functioning, and he has been able to get his driver's license and hold a great job. When he was early into his driver's education training, we'd practice in a parking lot and he'd ask, "Dad, how far do I turn the wheel to go around this corner?" and "How far should I press the gas pedal down?" He was looking for very specific answers. He wanted to know that he should turn the wheel to the two o'clock position and hold it there to make it around the island in the parking lot. At

---

first, I couldn't figure out how to help him understand that it's not that mechanical and you're always making adjustments. Finally, I said, "When you play Mario Kart, do you just hold the controller in one position?" He said, "No, of course not." I said, "That's right. You're using your eyes to sense how you're doing and you make little adjustments." He got it and that was all it took to get him over that hurdle.

Finding the pace of change that your company can accept is much like my son's situation. While we'd all like to know the number, it's not that simple. The best course is to choose a speed, get started, and use your senses to see, hear, and feel what is happening. From there, it's about never-ending course corrections. And just as with Mario Kart, practice will help you move faster and faster.

Focus on lasting gain

The ability of organizations to implement changes is strong, but the ability to sustain the changes is not nearly as robust. It reminds me of a great *Seinfeld* episode when Jerry was trying to rent a car. The dialogue goes like this:

Agent: May I help you? Name please?

Seinfeld: I made a reservation for a mid-size.

Agent: Okay, let's see here. Well, I'm sorry, we have no mid-size cars available.

Seinfeld: I don't understand. I made a reservation. Do you have my reservation?

Agent: Yes we do, but unfortunately we ran out of cars.

Seinfeld: But the reservation keeps the car here. That's why you have the reservation.

Agent: I *know* why we have reservations.

Seinfeld: I don't think you do. If you did, I'd have a car. See, you know how to *take* the reservation, but you just don't know how to *hold* the reservation, and that's really the most important part of the reservation.

The same could be said of most companies' attempts to change. They know how to *start* the change, but they don't know how to *hold* the change. I'd like to tell you that there's some magical pixie sustainment dust that you could buy on Amazon to make a change stick, but life doesn't work that way. Here are a few tips to improve your odds of success:

- Focus on the critical few—a recurring theme for execution.

- Embark on making the change with a plan for how to monitor and reinforce it. All habits require time to take hold.

- Win the war, not the battle. Remember why you're making the change and focus on the elements of the change that are critical. Don't be a purist about every nitpicky detail.

- Avoid chasing shiny objects. If you've done a good job of focusing on a critical area, then stick with it until the change is cemented before moving on.

- Reward and recognize change agents and teams for sustained results, not just for initiating change. Likewise, coach change teams to avoid "dump and run" tactics.

- When there is resistance to a change, walk a mile in the shoes of people living with the change. It's easy to dismiss resistance, saying "People are resistant to change." There are often very real issues that need to be addressed. If they aren't addressed, the change is likely to backslide.

Execute with Discipline: Changing Behaviors

"It is easier to act your way into a new way of thinking than to think your way into a new way of acting."
—Attributed to multiple sources

To execute with discipline, people will need to change. The exact formula for fixing each factory will be unique to the specific situation of that factory, but something will need to shift. Somebody—often many people—will need to do something different than they've done in the past, which means that we'll need to help them move toward the destination.

Note that I said that people would need to *do* something different. I didn't say that they will need to *think* something different. When we're implementing change, there will be a small subset who will naturally understand and embrace the change, but they will be the minority. For the vast majority of people, it will take some time after the change has been implemented to see a change in their mindset. Once they are living with the change for a length of time, they may start to change how they think about things.

Toyota does a great job of modeling this approach. They have an approach to problem-solving that the American press has described as Toyota Kata. A mentor will ask a mentee a series of questions as he is working on a problem:

1. What is the target condition?

2. What is the actual condition now?

3. What obstacles do you think are preventing you from reaching the target condition?

4. What is your next step? What do you expect?

5. When can we go and see what we have learned from taking that step?

After the mentee has experienced this line of questioning dozens of times, the thought process becomes natural. But Toyota only gets people to that point by having them repeat the behavior time and time again.

Getting buy-in

I do a fair amount of public speaking and one of the questions that I frequently get asked is, "How do I get people to buy in?" My flippant answer is, "You don't. You can try to perhaps get some to follow you, but most will not buy in until they see it working." As a leader, it's your job to get people through the journey and to the other side where they see the success. Once the success is staring them in the face, they'll proudly proclaim that they were on board from day one. What they are really saying is that they were on board from the day that it was an obvious success.

Every organization has a population of people that can be grouped into three categories:

Pioneers	These are the go-to people in an organization for every new initiative. They live for "new," and they enjoy being the point of the arrow. They blaze the trails. Usually, pioneers are about 15 percent of the population.
Settlers	The settlers are the biggest portion of the population—about 70 percent. They are more cautious about change and they wait for assurance that something new is going to work. They are calling out to the pioneers, asking, "Is it safe out there?"

CAVE People	The third group of people is the laggards and they represent about 15 percent of the workforce. The acronym C.A.V.E. stands for Citizens Against Virtually Everything. We all know who they are. They'd still use a rotary phone and VHS player if they were available. They move towards the future kicking and screaming.

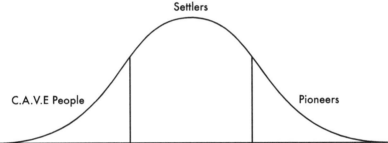

As a leader, where should you spend your time and energy? With the pioneers, settlers, or CAVE people? I suggest you should spend the preponderance of your time with the pioneers. Here's why.

When implementing change, there is a battle to win the hearts and minds of the settlers. The pioneers are saying, "Follow me," and the CAVE people are saying, "Don't go there, it's dangerous." When the change initiative encounters inevitable issues, the CAVE people put their recruiting engine into full speed, proclaiming "I told you so! I told you that wouldn't work! Come join me in the past!" What the settlers need to see is that the path being charted by the pioneers is safer and more fun, despite the short-term issues.

Pay attention to the pioneers. Give them most of your love and attention, especially when things aren't going well. Let the settlers see that the pioneers are getting rewarded and the CAVE people are getting ignored. Over time, the pioneers will make progress, the settlers will follow, and the CAVE people will either quit or grudgingly acquiesce. The whole curve will shift to the right and establish a new normal.

The Blue Whale and the Sardine

When there's a leadership change or different direction embarked upon, folks at your company may not be quick to embrace it right away. It's not uncommon and is often the natural course of things. But we can learn from nature, too. Take, for example, the story of the blue whale and a school of sardines.

The blue whale is the largest mammal on earth. At maturity, it can reach a length of 100 feet and weigh roughly 300,000 pounds. Let's put that in perspective. 100 feet is the height of a 10-story building. Go downtown and stand next to a 10-story building and imagine a living creature that size. And 300,000 pounds is nearly the weight of a Boeing 757. At birth, blue whales weigh close to two tons and grow about 200 pounds per day. It has a tongue the size of an elephant and a heart the size of a car. It makes me feel petite.

This gargantuan beast glides elegantly through the ocean, but it is not the nimblest of animals. It has a rigid body that prevents it from turning quickly (unlike a seal that has a flexible body). In fact, it takes two to three minutes for the blue whale to turn 180 degrees.

Contrast this with a school of sardines. Schools of sardines can exceed the size of the blue whale. Near Africa, sardines have been seen in groups upwards of seven kilometers long and two kilometers wide. While these schools are massive in their total size, they can shift direction with awesome speed and fluidity. Their ability to move as one unit has puzzled marine biologists. How do they do it? Do they communicate through sound, sight, or smell? Perhaps there is some sort of telepathic connection.

However, what scientists *have* found is that there is always a portion of the school that is swimming in a different direction than the prevailing flow. When that number of cross-swimming fish reaches a threshold, the whole school says, "This must be the way to go now," and they change direction. It doesn't take a majority of the fish to swim against the flow. In fact, it only takes 10 to 15 percent of them.

When I give speeches on effective leadership change, I'll often have an audience member ask, "How do I get everyone on board with the change?" My answer is you

> don't need to get everyone on board. You only need to get 15 percent of your team bought into the change and embracing the new path.
>
> Perhaps your company is a blue whale—large and slow to change. It doesn't need to be that way. Not everyone has to be completely receptive to the new direction right away. It only takes a few committed sardines to fight the trend and head in a different direction. The rest will follow.

We go backward before going forward

When we implement change, management's natural tendency is to focus on what needs to change and the benefits of doing so. We put together glossy PowerPoints that show what the future will look like and we describe the benefits and the road map. At the end of the presentation, when you expect everyone to be cheering and carrying you off on their shoulders, you see blank stares. You hear crickets. Maybe there's a question or two, but they have somewhat of a negative vibe. What happened? There's only upside to these changes. Why are they reacting this way?

Dick Hallstein, a well-respected coach on change, referred to this as the N-1 factor. "N" represents the current state. Management focuses on getting to N+1, some better future state. Management extols the benefits of N+1 and all the great things that will happen with it. Unfortunately, there is a natural human phenomenon of people not jumping to N+1. They don't even stay at N. They go to N-1—they go backward.

They don't go to N-1 because they oppose the future, but because they have some deep—but likely unspoken—concerns about how N+1 will affect them. Questions might include:

- Will I be competent?

- Who will be on my team and will I like them?

- Is my job secure?

- Who will eat lunch with me?

- Will my new boss honor my special work schedule agreement?

For the manager, there may be apparent answers. But if they are left unsaid, the employee is left to fill in the blanks. Most people fill those blanks with a negative bias, even to the point of catastrophizing.

One key to getting people moving towards N+1 is to think through the N-1 issues before announcing N+1. If you can guess what these concerns will be, you can answer them proactively as part of the rollout of the change. At a minimum, you'll demonstrate empathy and improve your connection with your employees. More likely, you'll significantly accelerate the commitment of your employees to the new plan. To move forward quickly, pause and reflect on the N-1 issues for your people.

Let's look at an example. Suppose that there is a contract manufacturing company that is under significant pricing pressure and to address it they have decided to implement Lean. Setup reduction is an area of emphasis. Historically, setups have taken a long time and are considered to be an art best left to master operators. The company sets a goal to reduce the setup time on one part from two hours to 10 minutes.

From a management perspective, this is a great goal. Waste is being eliminated so that the workers can concentrate on value-adding work. Costs will come down and product will flow to the customer better. In management's eyes, everyone wins. Leadership can have the best intentions, but consider how the artisan worker might feel and the questions he might have:

- Are they saying anyone can do what I do?

- If they're successful, are they going to replace me?

- It's a slap in the face to say that this can be done in 10 minutes. I'm the best operator here and I'm doing it as fast as I can. Are they saying that I'm incompetent?

- Are they going to expect me to train the new people so that they can eliminate my job?

- It's like they want to turn me into a robot.

- Running parts is boring. I like doing setups.

Once you've predicted some of the concerns of the workers, you can address them. It's great if you can eliminate the concerns, but even if you can't, acknowledging them will enable cooperation. Imagine if the leader sat down with the master operator and said this:

"Jim, I want to talk to you about an initiative we're launching. We want to reduce the setup time on Part ABC from about two hours to 10 minutes. I can imagine that this might raise some concerns for you. First, I want you to know that we picked this product on your line because of our respect for you. We know that you do the setup on this part as fast as anyone, but we want to push the limits of what can be done and learn some things that our competition can't do. In order to do that, we need your knowledge and wisdom. If this works, and we learn some new techniques, our thought is to have you take a lead role in rolling this out to other areas. I know that you don't get a lot of energy from just running parts, and you do enjoy the challenge of doing the set-ups. Great. We'd like to tap into that more and let others run the machine. What are your thoughts on getting engaged with this initiative?"

Taking the short amount of time to uncover and address the N-1 can do wonders to reduce the concerns of those who are most affected by the change. Organizations often talk about how their workforce is resistant change and that may be the case. However, the resistance is usually people being human and harboring natural fears and concerns. When management encounters resistance to N+1, it is time to step back, listen, and address the workers' N-1 concerns.

Turning anxiety into fear

There will be times when the changes that need to be implemented will have a negative impact on people. In this case, a leader's job is to turn our employees' anxieties into fears. This statement may sound unconventional—or even provocative—but I've found it to be true.

What's the difference between anxiety and fear? Fear has an object. You're afraid of something. Anxiety is a concern about the unknown. It often involves filling in the blanks and catastrophizing. The problem with anxiety is that we don't know what to do or how to respond. We freeze in a negative, destructive state with no path out. Fear is different. When we're afraid, we have clarity about what we're facing and we can start to make choices.

Let's look at an example of two people who are concerned about leaving their homes:

The first person has agoraphobia, which is an anxiety disorder. He is incredibly anxious about leaving the house but there is no reason for it. There's nothing tangible to fear, yet he harbors concerns about going out in the world. He is miserable and debilitated because his anxiety is unactionable.

The second person is afraid to go outside because there's a growling dog frothing at the mouth outside the front door. Now that he knows the nature of the problem, he can start asserting control and asking himself what to do. He can call animal control, wait it out, or make a run out the back door. The key is that he can start to determine how he wants to act, and that's a healthier mindset.

Shooting straight about bad news can feel uncomfortable and many leaders will want to wait until they have the answers to every question before talking with their people. Take an example of a department that is being shut down. Maybe during the Reveal the Issues stage, it was uncovered that a department was no longer competitive because the company hadn't invested in the right technology. It's a terrible situation and it's not the fault of the workers, but they're going to pay the price by losing their jobs.

Many leaders would want to keep the decision to close the department quiet until they knew exactly how it was going to unfold. They'd want to know who would keep their job, who would be let go, and the timing of the moves. As these plans are being developed, more people are brought into the planning process, and rumors start to leak on the floor. As the rumor mill gains speed, people fill in the gaps in the story with their own narrative and anxieties grow. By the time leadership announces the change, people are in a full-blown panic.

I think it's far better to communicate early, even if the eventualities are not known. There is a standard format for the meeting in which the difficult change will be announced:

1. State the reason for the meeting. E.g., We're here today because we have made the decision to close the XYZ department.

2. State the facts about what you know.

3. State what you don't know.

4. Tell them how you feel about the change. It's important for the leader to be genuine in their emotion. A supervisor might say, "Frankly, I'm angry about this. We warned the executives about the need for updated equipment for years and they didn't listen."

5. Describe the next steps and what they can expect from you.

This type of straightforward communication will start moving people from anxiety to fear. They now know the situation, at least as much as there is to know at the moment, and they can start taking control of their future.

During the Great Recession of 2008, when the housing market crashed, I was running a contract manufacturing company that sold 90 percent of its products to the housing industry. When housing crashed, volumes in the factory plummeted as well. I stood in front of all 300 employees and said, "I don't know how bad this is going to get, but I think it's likely that 50 percent of you won't be here six months from now. Since we're a union shop, we'll go by the rules of the agreement, so I think you can figure out who is likely to lose their job." I had a number of employees come up to me afterward and thank me for shooting straight and giving them some time to figure out what to do.

Communicating difficult news is not fun, but this is one of the responsibilities that you sign up for when you become a leader. Being direct and candid gives people the ability to control their future and it's the humane and caring way to handle the situation.

Changing norms of behavior

One of the most powerful forces that can inhibit the willingness and ability of people to change their behavior is the effect of groups. Humans are social creatures and we want to be part of a group and identify with that group. It may be a church group, sports team, work team, book club, or even a street gang.

Groups develop patterns and habits that form their norms of behavior. If someone violates these norms of behavior, they will get pressure from the group to get back in line. That pressure can be direct and vocal. It can also be more subtle.

The first factory that I worked in was an automotive parts manufacturer in Michigan. When a new worker would come in, they'd work on the line for a while, and if they were working at a fast pace a colleague would pull them aside and say, "Hey, slow it down, you're making us look bad." If the worker persisted, the pressure would increase, often isolating the person. People wouldn't talk to him or eat lunch with him. They might even spread vicious rumors about him. It was the very rare person who had will and strength to persevere through these pressures, and there were two common outcomes: the new hire would quit or conform.

The desire to be part of a group was demonstrated by an experiment conducted in 1951 by psychologist Solomon Asch. In the test, he assembled groups of seven students who had volunteered as test subjects into a room. He projected an image of four lines onto a wall. One line was the standard, and then there were three lines of differing lengths. The students were asked which of the three lines was the same as the standard. However, the deck was stacked. Six of the seven students were plants, and they were told which line to pick, and the seventh student was the real test subject. When the planted students gave the wrong answer, the test subject would also give the same wrong answer 37 percent of the time, even though they could clearly see that it was the wrong answer. This is both informative and perhaps a bit scary. The test subject had no affiliation with the other members of the group and he would receive no negative impacts for an answer that went against the group. Yet there was an innate desire to go along with the group.

Interestingly, they reran the experiment and just had one other person provide the right answer. Having just one other voice that agreed with the test subject's own observation dropped the number of incorrect answers to 5 percent. This study suggests that it does not take consensus or a majority to produce norm-breaking courage—it just requires that an individual does not feel completely alone.

Group norms of behavior are often described as "culture." They are the collective set of behaviors that are considered normal and accepted, and shifting these norms is extremely challenging. It's like a rocket trying to leave the orbit of the earth. It takes tremendous energy to pull away from the gravitational pull of the earth, and if the effort stops too early, the rocket plummets back down. Norms of behavior operate the same way. It takes steady, persistent effort to break from the gravitational pull of the old norm and create a new norm; if the effort stops too early, the old norm will cause the new behavior to crash and burn.

If fixing the factory requires a change in the norms of the group—a change in culture—then the leadership team has its work cut out for it.

Addressing Behavior Norms

When you are confronted with a behavior norm that you wish to change, you must be deliberate, focused, and resilient. I like to follow a four-step process:

1. Define the old and new behaviors

2. Unite leadership

3. Communicate the desired change and consequences

4. Spot check/Audit

1. Define the old and new behaviors

As the old saying goes, a well-defined problem is half-solved. It is worth the time and energy to explicitly state the behavior that you wish changed and what the preferred behavior is. This should be done as specifically as possible. For example:

Current behavior:

> Workers are waiting until the end of the shift to fill out the quality checklist.

Desired behavior:

> Workers fill out the quality checklist at the beginning, middle, and end of every lot. If the lot is not complete at the end of the shift, then the checklist should be completed at the end of the shift.

Examples of poor statements of behavior might be, "Improved attention to quality" or "Having a quality mindset," or even "Timely completion of checklists." It's important to state the behaviors that need to change. This is not about changing their "mindset," "attitude," "thought process," or "focus." This is about stating what we want the workers to *do*, not what we want them to *think*.

2. Unite leadership

Every leader at every level feels part of two teams. They feel like they are part of the team that they lead and they feel part of the team of their peers. Unfortunately in many companies, leaders feel much closer to the team they lead. In order to effectively change a behavioral norm, leaders must feel a closer connection with their peers than they do with their team.

The reason for this is simple. There will be group norms within the team and group norms among their peers. As you work to implement a behavioral change, particularly one that isn't liked, the team that a manager leads will exert the social pressures described earlier and there will be a strong pull to try to get the supervisor to succumb to the old behavior norm. However, if the leader has a stronger allegiance to his peer team, he'll have a safety net. While the team he is leading is exerting social pressures, his peer teams are welcoming and embracing him for conforming to their group norms.

The key to making this work is for the peer group to unite in their commitment to seeing the behavior change. This works best when the peer team meets together to talk about the current behavior and the desired behavior. They should openly discuss why the change is important, the likely resistance, and how they should handle situations where people are still doing the old behavior. This should be an open discussion so that issues can be vetted, discussed, and debated. It is the debate and feeling heard that helps the peer team solidify their resolve.

This dialogue is helpful even for minor changes. I was filling a leadership role at a plant on an interim basis, and one day when walking into the plant I noticed cigarette butts and other debris near the entrance to the plant. I don't know how many times I had walked past it without seeing it, but once I saw it I couldn't stop seeing. It may seem like a little thing, but I wanted the area cleaned up and I wanted it to stay clean. It's one of those little things that demonstrates that we really don't care and we're not disciplined. It is a small factor that is a strong indicator of pride in the company.

So, with a burr in my saddle I went to the production manager and asked, "What do we need to do to get the parking lot cleaned up and how do we get people to put the butts in the receptacle?" It irked me enough for me to shoot over the bow "If we can't make that happen, we'll just need to become a nonsmoking campus," which is where many companies have gone. This company may head that direction someday, but it shouldn't be because we couldn't figure out how to keep people from littering in the parking lot.

When this issue was raised with my leadership team, the floodgates opened and revealed a number of issues:

- We don't have receptacles on the way into the building.

- The smoking area is a long way from entry/exit.

- People aren't smoking in the right area anyway.

- People are smoking outside of the normal break times.

- The policy is clear, but we haven't been enforcing it. How do we deal with that?

- What about people who chew?

- What are we supposed to do if we see someone flick a butt onto the pavement?

We spent several hours discussing each of these concerns. We discussed the things that needed to be fixed before we attempted to adjust the behavior, and we reached agreement on how we would talk with people when they were sticking to the old behaviors. It was the dialogue, not the specific solutions, that generated alignment and commitment among the leadership team.

Some of the issues raised in this example may seem trivial, but they are important to the people trying to enforce the change. When you take the time to listen to these issues and work to answer questions, the first-line leaders will commit to the change because they feel armed to deal with it. They also know that their peers were part of the conversation and they are equally prepared to support the change.

There is no such thing as a small behavior change. If you want a change to stick, take the time to prepare and get the leadership team aligned and united.

3. Communicate the desired change and consequences

Implementing change without notifying people of the change isn't right or respectful.

Picture this scenario. You've been working as a mid-level manager for years. You've been getting steady raises and solid performance reviews. You come to work on Tuesday morning and your boss enters your office (with HR, I might add) to deliver a performance improvement plan (PIP). The reason for the PIP is because you didn't turn in your weekly report on Monday morning. You ask, "Weekly report? What is that? I've never done a weekly report." Your boss says, "It's in our management manual, in black and white, and you haven't been doing them. So, if you want to keep your job, you better toe the line and do them."

This sounds ludicrous, doesn't it? You had been doing just fine, and then without warning you're called out on something. And yet, this is how change is often carried out. Management wants a change, so they start "holding people accountable" to the new behavior without warning that a new behavior is even desired. We need to acknowledge that our past practices are the *real* policy manual. It doesn't matter what's written down. What matters is what has been practiced.

In order to elicit a behavioral change, we need to tell the workforce what we want and we need to acknowledge that it's different from past practices. That's only fair, and it's a sign of respect for people. This message works best when coupled with a strong "why" to indicate what is driving the change.

One element of the message to be communicated is the consequences of not adhering to the new behavior. Typically, this follows a progressive path that starts with coaching and perhaps retraining. From there, it escalates to disciplinary actions. That said, there will be times when you will want to adopt a zero-tolerance stance. A safety practice might be one of those times. Informing the team of the consequences will help them understand the seriousness of the new behavior.

4. Monitor frequently

For the new behavior to stick, it must be monitored and reinforced. The reinforcement can be both positive and negative. I prefer to focus on the positive reinforcement—catching people doing the desired behavior and providing positive feedback. That said, there may be a small portion of the population that will only respond to negative consequences.

The key is consistency and following through long enough to ensure the new behavior becomes the new norm. The rule of thumb is that it takes 20 days to establish a new habit. Personally, I think it takes longer. What's more, it takes continued monitoring, although that may become less frequent over time.

This is one of the most difficult aspects of any transformation. All systems display entropy—the gradual erosion into a state of disorder and randomness. The way to avoid this erosion is to continually monitor the systems and processes for signs of erosion and make immediate corrections. That sounds good, but businesses have hundreds, if not thousands, of processes and systems. How does one go about staying on top of all of them?

A common trap is for management to focus their energies on the latest change and lose sight of the other systems. This creates the program-of-the-month habit and the workforce becomes jaundiced and skeptical about all change initiatives. They know that management is going to hit the topic hard for a month, but then it will fade away and they can go back to the old way.

The solution is to have a balanced system that enables you to perpetually scan the environment, so you know when a process is beginning to erode. Key elements of the system include:

- The operating system discussed as a Core 10 process: The operating system has a regular meeting regimen with a scorecard that will let you know what things have started to go awry.

- Frequent listening and observation walks: These are more than quick walks down the aisles. They are intentional visits that give insight into the reality of the situation. If everyone on the leadership team, from the CEO to shop floor leads, are doing routine walks, then leadership will have a good, balanced view of what is happening on the floor.

- Standard work: Documenting the best-known process so that it can be observed is a key tool. When written well, standard work allows team leaders to watch the process to see if it's being performed according to the defined process. This will help leaders catch abnormalities early and make micro-corrections.

- Tier meetings and the daily management system: Strong local metrics reviewed every shift as part of a tier meeting structure can inform leaders about the erosion of processes.

Create wins

Winning creates engagement, not the other way around.

The conventional wisdom is that engagement comes first and high levels of engagement will lead to strong performance. When leaders believe that engagement comes first, they'll do things to create an atmosphere of engagement. This often means improved communication, recognition programs, idea boards, celebratory lunches, and supervisor development. These are attempts to win the hearts and minds of the workers. There is nothing wrong with these things, but they are missing the point. These efforts will be greeted with cynicism until the workforce sees some tangible evidence of improvement. They want to see wins, and when they do, these engagement tactics can play a vital supporting role.

We need to create some wins, however small, so the team starts to feel the energy that comes from positive results. Over time, as more and more wins are chalked up, there will be natural energy towards improvement. The team will thirst for it.

Consider visible high-performance teams like the New England Patriots. They are zealous about evaluating what they could do better. They review their gameplay, scrutinize their performance, and make adjustments. They are driven to do the extra work to be winners because they've experienced the sensation of winning and being the best.

I suppose that one could argue, "Give me a Tom Brady on my team and we'll do great, too." Even if you accept the argument that it takes star players to win, which I don't accept, it doesn't address the reality of the teams that we lead in our factories. The workforce is composed of average people. The goal of leadership is to get average people to do extraordinary things. One of the best ways to do that is to establish a pattern and expectation of winning. That will lead to continual learning and change to drive further improvement.

In *Good to Great*, Jim Collins introduces the concept of the flywheel effect. He describes a massive flywheel that initially takes tremendous energy to move just a little bit. However, with continued energy, the flywheel gets momentum and it begins to spin faster and faster. This is what it feels like with changes in the factory. In the early stages, every small change feels hard, but with each win the flywheel spins a little faster until improvement and winning become the norm.

Fixing a factory always involves changes, both large and small. The large initiatives tend to consume the attention of management, but companies will find that they can accelerate their improvement by getting all levels of the workforce involved in making improvements.

For example, take a contract manufacturer that has fallen behind on shipments to customers and they need to catch up. In order to do this, they need to increase their output by 20 percent. A first-line supervisor meets with his team and says, "In order to serve our customers well, we need to increase production by 20 percent. What ideas do you have?" Hopefully, the workers will offer ideas such as:

- The setup on Part A is taking way too long. I could use a fixture to drop that time and we might get an extra two hours per day off the machine.

- Our tool storage is a mess. I can't find what I need and I end up going to central stores to get replacements.

- The print for Part B is confusing. I've made two rejected weldments because of a misinterpretation of the print.

Individually, these items don't make a big dent in the overall goal of achieving the 20 percent throughput goal, but collectively they can add up. These small, local changes are victories and they create energy and engagement. It's contagious.

If a company has a history of blame and low trust, you can expect the process will start very slowly. That's okay. Grab one small thing. Go fix it in a way that doesn't blame anybody and celebrate the change. Rinse and repeat. Just keep doing it. You'll be pleasantly surprised by how quickly people will start to get energy from the improvements. The focus on making small, incremental improvements also helps supervisors get the knack of being proactive coaches as opposed to traditional, reactive, tyrannical foremen.

No doubt the key initiatives defined by the company are important, but those are the swing-for-the-fences initiatives. Let's get all of the workforce involved in singles and bunts. Home runs get the glory, but singles win the game.

Make it fun

A little fun can go a long way. I think we need to bring more joy and smiles to the workplace. Factories can have an atmosphere of being very workman-like and serious. We're always focused on production numbers, specifications, opportunities for improvement, root problem-solving, safety investigations, equipment breakdowns, part shortages, and so on. As a general theme, we are continually focused on what is wrong and what we need to do to fix it so that we can meet our objectives.

For some people, the focus on what is wrong and solving problems is truly energizing. It makes them come to work with a smile on their face because they get to go attack the next problem. For others, it gets to be a drag. Consider the way that we're taught to review scorecards. We scan the various metrics and if they are on target we skip over them so we can focus on the ones that are off target. That makes sense from the perspective of managing time, but it's also deflating that we take almost no time to celebrate our victories and have some fun. Over time, it can feel like all management is doing is pointing out everything we're doing wrong.

I understand that good leaders don't intend this outcome, but it can happen. We need to provide a counterbalance that brings some levity, joy, and humanity into the workplace. The kinds of things that can be done are limited only by your imagination: pizza parties, a BBQ with management serving the meal, dress-up days, an applause ceremony for the best ideas of the month, mini-contests, charitable causes, book clubs over lunch, bell ringing when milestones are met, and the list goes on. In one factory, an employee put Christmas lights and tinsel on a forklift and drove through the factory handing out candy canes.

Fun means different things to different people. Some people like quirky and silly things, others like contests and competitions, and others consider quiet things to be fun. For me, "fun" is my dog and I on the lake doing a little bass fishing. I'm a proud introvert. My point is that there is a wide range of things that bring joy to people and make them smile.

Practice doing some lighthearted activities that bring a smile to people's faces. I understand that manufacturing is a serious business, but people will be prepared to enter the difficult activities when they have high energy and uplifted spirits.

Changing behaviors: Wrap-up

I've spent a lot of time discussing the people component of executing with discipline and that was intentional. Leading people through change is one of the largest factors that will determine your success. Building an environment of respect and trust with empathy and compassion is rocket fuel for your business. Place your focus on changing behaviors, not minds, and put yourself in the shoes of those being affected. Your team is not a bunch of robots they're much better than that. Meet them where they're at and lead them.

Executing with Discipline: Wrap-up

When I first started writing this section, I called it "Executing with Precision." I scratched that idea because it doesn't address the reality of what it really feels like to lead a factory out of distress towards health and stability.

It's a messy, emotional process. There are the rewarding days when you can see the progress being made and there are the days when nothing seems to be going right. It will test your mettle, but it will be worth it.

Great ideas alone won't fix a factory. Improvement only happens when ideas are turned into reality and that requires disciplined execution.

WRAP-UP: REFLECTIONS BEFORE MOVING FORWARD

"The world breaks everyone, and afterward,
some are strong at the broken places."
—*Ernest Hemingway*

Factories are complicated machines. Over decades, manufacturers have honed the techniques for making factories work and we see the fruits of those labors all around us. However, even the best factories will go through periods where things don't work the way they should. It is sometimes surprising to see how quickly things can go awry when one small cog in the machine isn't working well. Factories are much like cars. They are high-performance machines that run great until they don't. Sometimes the issues are minor like a clogged fuel filter or a dead battery. Other times, the issues are larger, like an engine that is worn out and needs an overhaul.

In *How to Fix a Factory*, I've provided a roadmap for getting a factory running again. There are five basic steps:

1. Set the Stage

2. Reveal the Issues

3. Reset Expectations

4. Prioritize the Core 10 Systems

5. Execute with Discipline

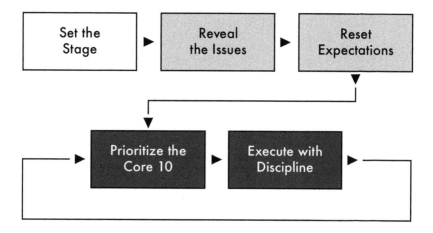

Following this roadmap will dramatically reduce the time that it takes to get back on stable footing.

When factories are working well, everyone benefits. Customers are getting the products that they need. Workers have employment stability and are engaged in being part of the business. Owners are seeing financial returns that they deserve for their investments, and the community-at-large is reaping the benefits of being part of the factory ecosystem.

I want North American manufacturing to succeed and the best way to make that happen is to have successful factories. When factories are successful, boards and owners will be relieved of the pressure to look outside of the company for solutions. They won't feel the need to move to a low-cost country, outsource production, or close the business.

All manufacturing companies need fixing to one degree or another, and it starts by taking stock of the current situation. I've compiled a list of 20 questions to spur your thought process. This is not a scientific, numerically precise, calibrated assessment. Rather, it is intended to help you reflect and uncover the degree to which your factory may need tuning up. I recommend that you respond to each statement yourself and then provide a copy of the questionnaire to your team and have them complete it. Review the results together as a leadership team. It should help you arrive at insights about your areas of strength, as well as those areas that may need attention.

1) The company produces consistent, predictable, positive financial results.

Strongly Disagree	Disagree	Neutral	Agree	Strongly Agree
1	2	3	4	5

2) Managing the company feels stable (not chaotic).

Strongly Disagree	Disagree	Neutral	Agree	Strongly Agree
1	2	3	4	5

3) Our customers feel that we serve them well.

Strongly Disagree	Disagree	Neutral	Agree	Strongly Agree
1	2	3	4	5

4) Our employees are engaged, and they come to work for much more than a paycheck.

Strongly Disagree	Disagree	Neutral	Agree	Strongly Agree
1	2	3	4	5

5) The entire organization is focused on the critical few initiatives that will move the needle.

Strongly Disagree	Disagree	Neutral	Agree	Strongly Agree
1	2	3	4	5

6) The company generates financial results that satisfy ownership and allows for adequate reinvestment in the business.

Strongly Disagree	Disagree	Neutral	Agree	Strongly Agree
1	2	3	4	5

7) We can hire and retain the workforce that we need today and for the future.

Strongly Disagree	Disagree	Neutral	Agree	Strongly Agree
1	2	3	4	5

8) The workplace is safe and clean, and we take pride in keeping it that way.

Strongly Disagree	Disagree	Neutral	Agree	Strongly Agree
1	2	3	4	5

9) Our equipment is reliable and maintained well.

Strongly Disagree	Disagree	Neutral	Agree	Strongly Agree
1	2	3	4	5

10) The supply base is aligned with our needs, and they serve us well.

Strongly Disagree	Disagree	Neutral	Agree	Strongly Agree
1	2	3	4	5

11) We have appropriate inventory levels that are well organized and controlled.

Strongly Disagree	Disagree	Neutral	Agree	Strongly Agree
1	2	3	4	5

12) We do a good job of aligning the sales forecast with the operations and financial plan.

Strongly Disagree	Disagree	Neutral	Agree	Strongly Agree
1	2	3	4	5

13) We have good data and metrics to run the business.

Strongly Disagree	Disagree	Neutral	Agree	Strongly Agree
1	2	3	4	5

14) We are effective at implementing the company strategy.

Strongly Disagree	Disagree	Neutral	Agree	Strongly Agree
1	2	3	4	5

15) Everyone in the company knows our values, and we live by them.

Strongly Disagree	Disagree	Neutral	Agree	Strongly Agree
1	2	3	4	5

16) We have effective meetings.

Strongly Disagree	Disagree	Neutral	Agree	Strongly Agree
1	2	3	4	5

17) All employees know the company strategy and their role in implementing it.

Strongly Disagree	Disagree	Neutral	Agree	Strongly Agree
1	2	3	4	5

18) Continual change and improvement is normal, and we're good at it.

Strongly Disagree	Disagree	Neutral	Agree	Strongly Agree
1	2	3	4	5

19) Our employees feel that they have a voice and they feel respected.

Strongly Disagree	Disagree	Neutral	Agree	Strongly Agree
1	2	3	4	5

20) The changes that we implement stick and generate positive results.

Strongly Disagree	Disagree	Neutral	Agree	Strongly Agree
1	2	3	4	5

The maximum score on this self-assessment is 100. How did your company fare? My guess is that you didn't get fives across the board. I know that I've never seen a manufacturer that can answer all of these with an honest five. If you scored 75 or better, you likely have a factory that is healthy but in need of improvement in a couple of areas. A score of 50 to 75 is a fragile factory that may be tipping towards unhealthy. A score of 50 or less is an indication that the factory is struggling, and aggressive intervention may be appropriate.

When areas are weak, act to make them better. Use the concepts discussed in this book to focus on a few critical initiatives and guide your people through the change. Execute with discipline. You will be stronger as a result, and then you can move on to the next improvement.

What Success Feels Like

I have had the good fortune to be associated with some companies that have crossed the chasm from troubled to healthy. Working in a company that is healthy and winning is an immensely satisfying experience.

When I was the CEO at Intek Plastics, I experienced this firsthand. In my early days there, we were struggling. Financial performance was weak. Customers were frustrated with our value proposition and the relationship with the unionized workforce was confrontational. After three years of very heavy lifting, things were in a much better place. With one major customer, we advanced from being on double-secret probation to becoming their number one supplier. Profits had reached healthy levels that satisfied the shareholders. However, the most rewarding aspect to me was the renewed spirit of the workforce. There are two stories that come to mind.

I was walking the shop floor one summer day, and the chief shop steward of the union pulled me aside and asked if we could talk. He asked me if the company was okay. I was puzzled, and replied, "Sure, things are great. Why do you ask?" He said, "It seems too slow out here. People are worried. This is our busy season. It's supposed to be nuts, chaotic." I told him that we were having record sales with record production levels and that we're growing and hiring. He just looked at me and said, "I suppose this is how it's supposed to feel, eh?" He had a small smile on his face and just turned and went back to work. I also had a smile on my face as I continued the tour.

The other story involved a visitor touring the factory. We were considering switching accounting firms and I toured the head of the manufacturing practice through the facility. He had been on hundreds of shop floors and he had a deep understanding of what good manufacturers look like. When we were done, he said, "Rob, you have something special going on here." I said, "I think so," and I started to rattle off some of the improvements we made. He said, "Those are good, but I'm talking about the energy on the floor. You can feel it. I could see it in the way people made eye contact with you and the bounce in their step. Did you know that three people called you over to show you an improvement that they had been working on?" At the time, I didn't realize what we had going was special, but I can see it now. People were engaged and energized. It was palpable and real.

Both of these anecdotes give insight into what it feels like when factories have foundational health. Work isn't something that you dread. It's a part of your life that provides intrinsic value and growth. Getting to this point takes hard work and perseverance, but it is possible and worth the journey.

I wish you the best as you work to improve your factory. Be strong, stay focused, respect your people, and be a leader.

ACKNOWLEDGEMENTS

I am grateful to all of the people who have mentored me over the years—John Penn, Dick Krant, Pat Riley, Erik Skie, Dick Hallstein, Jim Cutler, and my dad. These people invested their time and energy to help me grow as a person and a professional, and I am indebted to them. The insights from these people are woven throughout this book.

I am also appreciative of all of the people who have taken the time to commit their ideas to paper. I'm a prolific reader, and great authors like Dr. Jeff Liker, Tom Peters, Jim Collins, and Seth Godin have all shaped my perspective.

I would love to list all of the people who I have worked with over the years, but the list would be too long. While books can provide an academic perspective on the world, it was the daily interactions with each of you that kept me grounded.

Sarah Parker, my writing coach, deserves special acknowledgement. She guided me through the writing process, supporting me when I was discouraged and giving me a gentle prod when it was needed. Sarah—thank you for helping me to find my voice.

Finally, I want to thank my wife, children, mom, and dad. Without their love and support, I would never have had the courage to take on this challenge.